Endorsements

All effective board members make great preparations. For anyone aspiring to get that coveted board position, preparation is key. From understanding the needs of the board to assessing your own fit and standing out above the crowd, *Board Ready* will help you traverse this journey.

—Diane Ballantyne
Councillor and Active Board Member

Debra and David Brown have written a practical, understandable, step-by-step guide for anyone wanting to serve as a board member. Their unique inside perspective on how boards develop profiles, interpret them, and assess candidates will give you a leg up toward preparing for, finding, and responding to board opportunities.

—Tim Foster
Chair of Directors' Forum Cooperative and Former Chair of Northern Credit Union

Board Ready is a tremendous help for people seeking a seat on a board and who have questions or may be nervous about it. It is a useful guiding light for any aspiring board member. I know they will be immensely grateful for the advice.

—Holly Skinner
Community Advocate and Aspiring Board Member

Every prospective board member should read this clear and useful explanation of how to get a seat on a board. The dynamics of board succession are changing. Today's boards are looking for specific talents and attributes, not just CEO's. This book shows you what boards want and need, how to become board-ready, and gives practical steps for targeting your response to get your seat at the table.

—Leanne Bellegarde, K. C.

Board Ready is the essential guide for being ready to take your seat at the table. This step-by-step guide by Brown & Brown gives you a thoughtful approach to getting a board position. I particularly appreciated the valuable examples and sample board résumé that will help you get started on your journey.

—George Prudat
Chair, North West College and Saskatchewan Research Council,
Former Mayor, and Commander, Royal Canadian Navy

BOARD READY

HOW TO SECURE YOUR SEAT ON THE BOARD
OF DIRECTORS TO MAKE AN IMPACT,
ADVANCE YOUR CAREER, AND GROW YOUR INCOME

BOARD READY

HOW TO SECURE YOUR SEAT ON THE BOARD OF DIRECTORS TO MAKE AN IMPACT, ADVANCE YOUR CAREER, AND GROW YOUR INCOME

DR. DEBRA L. BROWN AND
DAVID A. H. BROWN

ethos
collective

Printed in the United States of America

Published by Igniting Souls
PO Box 43, Powell, OH 43065
IgnitingSouls.com

LCCN: 2024911055
Paperback ISBN: 978-1-63680-304-3
Hardcover ISBN: 978-1-63680-305-0
e-book ISBN: 978-1-63680-306-7

Available in paperback, hardcover, e-book, and audiobook.

To the hundreds of Professional Directors® who have trusted us to help them in their journey to become and remain board ready!

With special thanks to our contributing authors and team members Sarah Hall, Rob DeRooy, and Vicki Dickson, and those on the Governance Solutions Team who made this book possible: Ana Almeida, Tan Crombie, Rafael Mazotine, Dave McComiskey, and Jake Skinner

Table of Contents

Introduction

For plenty of executives, a board seat is an aspirational goal. There's the money, of course. The average total director compensation was $321,220, according to the 2023 U.S. Spencer Stuart Board Index.[1] But the benefits fall across a cascade of other categories for professionals who manage to secure that coveted position.

It's a big career boost. Research published in the Harvard Business Review[2] found that when an executive snags a board seat, they are 44 percent more likely to be promoted as a first-time CEO to an S&P 1500 firm. And even if they don't get that promotion, their annual pay goes up by 13 percent.

Serving on a board is an opportunity to cycle off the daily grind of C-suite life. If you're inclined to walk away from the day-to-day work of running a company, a board seat is a great way to put your skills to work without the constant stress of a full-time leadership role.

And it's a chance to give back. With years of experience, you now have a chance to guide and advise everybody, from burgeoning startups eager for a steady hand to generations-old corporations that need to pivot to address today's challenges.

Ready to sign up? We've got good and bad news.

The bad news is this: Securing a board seat often involves a highly competitive process that culminates after years of networking.

And the good news: As they hunt for their next board member, today's companies are seeking depth and breadth in experience and perspective.

Today's boards don't just want a generic "leader." As the world gets more complicated, companies need experts in everything from technology and digital transformation to global business practices and equity, diversity, and inclusion on their boards.

And, as a response to global social justice movements and to ensure companies are serving increasingly diverse consumer bases, they're on the lookout for board members from all backgrounds. According to Spencer Stuart 2023 Board Index, the diversity of S&P 500 board members is on the rise. Some 75 percent of new first-time directors are from traditionally underrepresented groups, including women and people of color—up from 39 percent in 2013.

But just because corporations have opened their boardroom doors wider, getting a seat is still no walk in the park. For those just beginning their journey, the process can seem shrouded in mystery. Take heart: Somewhere out there is an organization that needs your expertise and perspective, and there are steps you can take right now to set yourself up for success.

Here at Governance Solutions, we know what it's like to be in your shoes. Through our Professional Director Education and Certification Program®, we've worked with hundreds of aspiring board members just like you. Once they graduated, they were ready and eager to serve but couldn't find a spot that was right for them.

Frankly, they reminded us a little bit of our son back when he was 16, frustrated he didn't have a job. He had the skills required to work at a local sandwich shop, but he spent most of his time playing guitar in his bedroom. He wasn't taking the active steps required to connect with employers and get a job.

Same goes for aspiring board members. To get that board seat, credentials aren't enough. You have to get out there. You have to determine what companies need and how your unique experience and perspective can solve their problems.

In this book, we will reveal the secrets to obtaining a seat on a board. Based on a series of workshops our company has given titled "How to Get a Seat on the Board: Four Steps to Your Dream Board," each chapter will give you the knowledge and tools required to find opportunities and sell yourself as the right candidate.

Here's what we'll cover:

Chapter One: How to uncover and understand what boards want and need.

We'll dive into who boards are looking for and how to zero in on positions that are best for you.

Chapter Two: How to get the board's attention.

It's all about networking—at conferences and meetings and, especially now, online. We'll light the way forward.

Chapter Three: How to be the perfect match.
We'll focus on what it takes to craft the perfect board résumé to ensure it matches what the board is looking for.

Chapter Four: How to make an impression and a connection.
We'll show you how to nail the interview by doing the right research and preparation.

Now it's time for you to take that first step. Turn the page to get board ready and start your journey to the board seat you've always wanted.

1

What Boards Want

Today's boards are looking for specific talents and attributes, not just CEOs.

—*Dr. Debra L. Brown*

Not that long ago, it was easy to figure out who board members were looking for when they needed somebody new to join their fold. It was their friend at the golf course. Their old college buddy. A former co-worker. They looked to people in their network who had risen to the C-suite in their respective companies, often CEOs. And that was enough.

For decades, boards filled vacant seats through personal connections. And, because of longtime practices and biases that have made it essentially impossible for women and people of diverse ethnicities, backgrounds, and experiences to rise through the ranks, new board members looked no different than the board members they replaced: They were pretty much all white men.

For all the right reasons, the path to the boardroom is different today. No longer is it exclusively an enclave for older white male executives. Increasingly, the faces in boardrooms are reflective of the diverse world we live in.

The progress is glacial, but there's been some improvement. Among Fortune 500 companies in 2020, more than half had boards that were composed of more than 40 percent women and people of color, according to a report by the Alliance for Board Diversity and Deloitte.[3]

And a StatsCan report[4] released in early 2021 found that government business entities and publicly traded companies had the highest shares of women on boards—more than one-third and 23 percent, respectively. But, on privately held boards, less than one in five directors were women.

Over the decades, the desire to build more diversity on boards has been a nice-to-have strategy—often a gesture of goodwill. These days, it's simply a smart business decision.

That's because investors are demanding diversity. Recently, in fact, a major investor in a private sector company we work with threatened to leave the company if the organization didn't recruit more women to their board. The threat of losing their significant investors prompted them to up their game.

Regulators are requiring it. There's been some legislative pressure in Europe[5] and in California[6] and at NASDAQ to reach gender parity. Canada, however, is unlikely to legislate it anytime soon.

And consumers and clients that companies are serving are more diverse themselves and bring buying power that can make or break organizations. Minority buying power across the United States has exploded—up from $458 billion in 1990 to $3 trillion in 2020, according to the University of Georgia's Selig Center for Economic Growth's 2021 Multicultural Economy report[7]. Asian Americans, African Americans, and Hispanics "wield formidable economic clout," according to the report.

Organizations that capitalize on all this diversity—hiring a diverse workforce and bringing on diverse leadership—are more innovative and successful, according to McKinsey & Co[8]. It makes sense. When your workforce and leadership reflect your customer base, you're harnessing the very perspectives and ideas of the people you're selling your products and services to.

Diversity: Background + Experience

Diversity of background is one piece to the puzzle as boards select new members. So is *diversity of experience.* The business world is far more complicated than it was even two decades ago, and boards need the knowledge and experience of subject matter experts.

Technology has transformed the way we do everything—at home and at work. Drones are delivering packages, and robots are taking over tasks on factory floors. Artificial intelligence is augmenting the work of us humans. And machine learning is making it possible to gain new insights into trends and operations that will drive business in new directions. As organizations design their own digital transformation, they need tech experts in the boardroom who understand the potential of existing and emerging technologies.

What's more, the workforce demands new action and focus. Long after the so-called Great Resignation amid the COVID-19 pandemic, workers have made it clear that they're no longer interested in just a paycheck. They are seeking jobs where their work is valued and they have opportunities to grow and develop. Meanwhile, social justice issues are putting equity, diversity, and inclusion (EDI) initiatives into greater focus. Boards need human resources experts who can navigate these new needs and expectations.

Even risk is considered from a different viewpoint as organizations adopt ESG, or environmental, social, and governance, goals. Many leaders are starting to understand that addressing the climate crisis, diversity in their workforce, and the ethics behind their policies and practices may take time and money, but it can cost an organization even more if they overlook them.

Some 85 percent of investors consider ESG factors as they look at opportunities, according to Gartner.[9] And 77 percent of consumers say they are motivated to buy from companies that are committed to making the world a better place, according to a survey by AFLAC.[10] Boards need members who understand ESG best practice and can ensure organizations are meeting the expectations of investors and customers.

In other words, while the general business expertise of a CEO might have been enough for boards a generation ago, it isn't anymore. Boards need a broad range of executives with very specific expertise to help address and oversee the complicated nature of today's business decisions.

That's why companies are increasingly laser-focused on building a board that acts as a collective mind—where each individual represents distinct interests, competencies, and skills that, as a whole, provide the know-how, wisdom, and innovative insights required to successfully lead in this fast-changing environment.

All these factors are helping to fling the boardroom doors open for new entrants who have the right set of skills, character, and diversity of thought. But it also makes the process of finding a board seat more complicated. That's why understanding how boards select members and the factors that drive their decisions is critical so you can best position yourself for a seat.

Here are the steps that boards take as they search for new directors and how they reveal the skills and competencies they need.

Step 1: Assessing Board Needs

As board seats open up, board members typically run through a series of exercises to determine the experience, skills, knowledge, education, and diversity of those who remain at the table and the gaps they need to fill because of the current exit.

But, as business needs shift, boards often don't want to replace a board member with somebody with the very same knowledge. To meet a company's long-term goals, they may need to bring somebody in with expertise they never needed before—perhaps business experience in Asia or a retention expert to shore up growing turnover rates.

As board members consider the gaps they need to fill, here are some of the questions they often ask themselves.

- **What are the key objective areas?**
  - o Are they looking to diversify the board?
  - o Are they grappling with specific issues that a subject matter expert could help oversee?
  - o Are they planning to expand into a new geographic area?

- **Where has the company been, and where is it going?**
  - o What strategies were successful, and what needs to be shored up?

o What are the organization's future plans, and in what areas do they have experience or leadership gaps?

- **What knowledge, experience, skills, and education are needed?**

  o What's the background of the current board members?

  o What are the gaps that need to be filled?

- **What diversity and representational affinities should be considered?**

  o What is the diversity of the ownership, consumer, and client base?

  o How diverse is the workforce?

  o Do current board members reflect that level of diversity?

- **What character expectations are required?**

  o Are good listening skills, being a team player, integrity, and collegiality, for example, important?

  o What are the company culture and values, and how should board members live them out?

Step 2: Candidate Skills Matrix

Board members obviously need to be smart, experienced, and focused. They need to have turned their intelligence into wisdom and have the ability to oversee rather than operate. But boards often require so much more as they look for the right candidates.

Once boards have evaluated themselves and their needs, they develop a matrix to rate the candidates in three primary areas—their competencies, their character, and their diversity.

Three Primary Areas Boards Will Consider

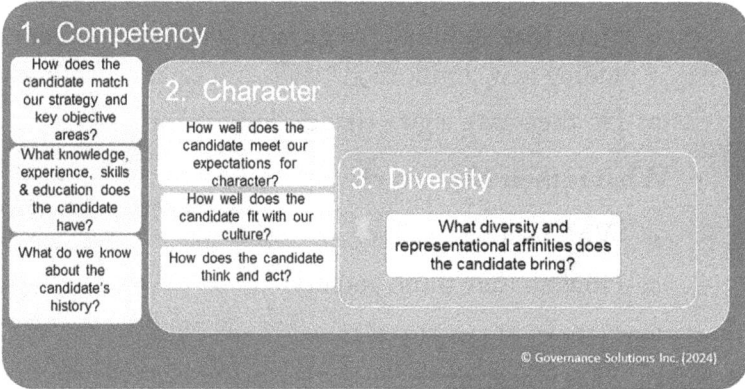

1. Competency

How does the candidate match our strategy and key objective areas?

What knowledge, experience, skills & education does the candidate have?

What do we know about the candidate's history?

2. Character

How well does the candidate meet our expectations for character?

How well does the candidate fit with our culture?

How does the candidate think and act?

3. Diversity

What diversity and representational affinities does the candidate bring?

© Governance Solutions Inc. (2024)

Résumé Reflections on Competencies

First, board members consider the facts—the objective qualifications of any candidate that might be listed in a résumé, on LinkedIn, or another online profile.

- **What industries have they worked in?**
  - o Is it relevant to the organization's needs?
  - o Or would a leader from another industry bring the kind of fresh ideas required for an expected pivot?

- **To what level of depth have they worked in those particular industries?**
  - o Have they moved from industry to industry, or have they stuck it out in a specific field? Does that matter?
  - o What have they achieved?

- **What are the skills that they've learned along the way?**

  o Do those specific competencies mesh with the needs of the organization going forward?

- **What's their education?**

  o Have they continued to grow in their development, adding new certifications, skills, or degrees over time?

  o Do they have a governance designation?

- **What is their character?**

  o Who are they really?

  o How do they think and act?

Character Considerations

Candidates, of course, aren't just evaluated based on their résumé. Character considerations are critical too. As boards build a matrix for evaluating candidates, they'll consider what character traits are most important to them. Especially as more organizations adopt ESG factors that require leaders to govern with integrity, it's likely character considerations will play an even greater role in board deliberations about prospective members.

Of course, measuring how forthright and ethical a person is isn't as easy as calculating the length of their career. These qualities are most often revealed in interviews, recommendations, social media posts, and media interviews. As candidates build their own stories about themselves, they must think about how their interactions with others online and in person demonstrate how they walk in the world and treat others with respect and integrity.

Diversity Deliberations

As we've already spelled out, diversity of background and experience is critical these days. For every reason, boards are focused on building diversity across an organization—including in the boardroom. And, if they haven't gotten to it first, stakeholders, including investors and customers, may threaten to walk away if they don't take action.

A candidate's skills will always be the most important—that diversity of experience that they bring. A board won't completely favor diversity of background over competency. But boards are starting to balance the scales. After generations of white men having a leg up simply because of who they were, board members who are considering two candidates with equal experience may opt for the candidate who brings some level of diversity to the table. And, in some cases, some boards are *only* looking at candidates who will enhance the visible diversity of their board—and, of course, bring the required competencies and character too.

Insider's View: Weighting Candidates

When we help clients analyze board candidates, we often use a chart like this to organize an analysis of their skills and attributes. In this case, we started with several résumés and narrowed them down based on their match with the organization's competencies and skills gaps. Finally, we interviewed the five people who best matched those gaps. Not every board will score candidates in this way, but it's a common method for sifting through applicants.

Weighting Candidates

Interview Rankings

Candidate	Interviewer A	Interviewer B	Interviewer C	Interviewer D	Average Total Score
Candidate 1	89	125	105	109	107
Candidate 2	96	88	102	90	94
Candidate 3	78	92	99	93	90.5
Candidate 4	92	72	83	95	85.5
Candidate 5	82	90	56	74	75.5

Attributes and Competencies Gap Analysis

	Candidate 1	Candidate 2	Candidate 3	Candidate 4	Candidate 5
Level 1: Where have you been? Industry Knowledge and Experience (Rating from 1 – 5 with 5 being the highest)					
Industry Experience	5	4	5	3	5
Financial/Accounting Expert	4	4	5	1	5
Talent Management and Executive Compensation Expert	2	3	4	5	4
Digital Business	5	2	2	2	2
Level 2: What Do You Know? Functional Skills Competencies (Rating from 1 – 5 with 5 being the highest)					
Audit & Compliance	3	2	5	3	4
Financial Literacy	4	4	5	4	5
Corporate Governance & Ethics	5	5	3	3	4
Leadership & Executive Management	5	5	4	5	5
Regulatory Environment	5	4	4	4	4
Risk Management Oversight	5	4	4	4	4
Strategic Planning	5	5	4	4	4
Mergers & Acquisitions	5	3	5	3	4
Level 3: Affinities and Diversity					
Gender Diversity	Female	Male	Male	Trans	Female
Visible Diversity	Yes	No	Yes	No	Yes
Geographic Diversity	North	North	South	East	Central
Level 4: Education					
Post-Secondary	MBA	MBA	BA	BA	PHD
Other Education	Yes	No	No	Yes	Yes
Governance Designation (e.g. Pro.Dir. (Professional Director) or other recognized governance designation.)	Yes	Yes	No	No	No
Level 5: Character Attributes (Rating from 1 – 5 with 5 being the highest)					
Ethical	5	4	5	5	4
Constructive Communicator	5	4	4	4	5
Commitment and Engagement	5	4	4	4	5
Independent Fiduciary	4	5	5	5	5
Emotionally Mature	5	5	4	4	5
Strategic Thinker	5	5	5	5	5
Wise	5	5	4	4	5

Here's how it works.

First Round: Competencies

In the first round, résumés are evaluated, looking for the key competencies that the board requires. Each competency has a specific definition that's typically available for viewing via an online posting or ad.

For example, a board may not just be seeking someone with board experience. They may be seeking someone with board experience, including board or committee leadership roles, in a publicly traded corporation in the financial services sector with over $20 billion in assets. Boards often will be very specific in their ads and postings, spelling out exactly what they need.

Takeaway: Just like on the job hunt, you likely won't check yes on every single requirement for a board seat. The perfect fit is exceedingly rare. It's unlikely there are many people who have served in both senior IT and HR roles, for example. As you peruse board member listings, don't be discouraged if you have little experience in one or two of the categories. Your application is about showing off the expertise that you do have.

Second Round: Attributes

Then, we look at attributes that aren't listed or may not be obvious on a résumé—character, soft skills, and diversity. This will include conducting internet searches, checking social media, and looking for news articles about the candidate. Those individuals short-listed from their résumé are interviewed, delving into character considerations and cultural fit. In some cases, geography matters. For example, some boards seek candidates from a certain city, province, or state where their company is based.

Takeaway: Not every board will make the extra effort to check out candidates through online searches. Your résumé may be the only way to demonstrate your character and diversity. Find a way to weave that information in by including aspirations, awards, memberships, or volunteer work, for example.

Final Calculations: Weighting

In each round, candidates are rated against their different competencies and attributes—typically awarding ratings based on a scale of one to five. Rankings are multiplied by the weight of each category. Some boards add all these ratings together to give each candidate an overall number, which becomes their final ranking. There is a big caution to keep in mind here. The board is attempting to fill any competency gaps they may have on their board, so they will consider yours against those gaps. For example, it may not matter that you have expertise in financial oversight if they already have five accountants on their board. You may get bonus marks if you do bring that experience, but if they really need a human resources oversight expert, that is where they will focus. Or, if there were two similar candidates and one brought some of the diversity that the board had defined, that candidate would get a little boost.

Takeaway: Each competency and attribute is not weighted equally. Using objective weighting helps to remove recruiter biases and equalizes candidates on those factors that are measurable.

Final Analysis

Here are some key lessons for prospective board members:

1. Character Matters

More than ever, character—the moral and mental foundations of each individual—matters in today's business world and boardrooms. You can train for competencies like industry experience or corporate history and strategy. But it is almost impossible to train for character during a board member's tenure. Character is built over a lifetime, not over a three to six-year stint on a board.

When a board member lacks character, the risks are great. At the very least, weak character traits will sour team cohesion. At the very worst, the risks to organizational reputation are vast. Abraham Lincoln, the sixteenth president of the United States, is famously quoted as saying, "People think the real test of a person's character is how they deal with adversity, but a much better test of a person's character is how they deal with power. I've been more disappointed with how the character of people is revealed when they have been given power."

As organizations seek to find competent, courageous, inclusive, equitable, honest, and upright leaders to serve on their boards, they're looking for people who will lead with impeccable character, integrity, and respect.

Character matters and must be developed.

2. Image Matters

Board members will be mindful of candidates' personal brand and image. And with social media platforms and online searches, it's easier than ever to uncover how individuals are perceived in the public eye. As we'll cover more in the next chapter, think about your authentic self, and protect your brand by refraining from posting inappropriate or offensive content on LinkedIn and elsewhere.

Search firms, evaluators, and potential boards are watching. In a recent board search we conducted, based on her résumé, the top-rated candidate on our list seemed to be the perfect fit. In fact, she significantly outscored the rest of the pack. But she never made it to the interview stage.

It did not take much for an online scan to discover a speech she had given a few months earlier. She had been highly critical of a number of the other individuals currently serving on the very board she was hoping to get the seat on. Someone had posted a video of her speech on YouTube. This discovery not only closed the door on her chances to get on this board, but her very public negative comments shed light on character traits that caused us to reject her as a candidate for any other board seat opportunities that could come up in the future.

Image matters and must be protected.

3. Education Matters

Advanced degrees, industry-specific certifications, and top-notch professional experience are expected among prospective board members. But that's not all that successful candidates must bring.

You should also demonstrate a life-long love of learning, whether it's through those advanced degrees and new certifications or a clear desire to understand emerging technologies, market needs, or societal trends. Great board members are ready and eager to learn and bring the critical-thinking skills required to understand all sides of an issue and make smart, nuanced decisions.

Education matters and your love of learning must be evident.

4. Governance Matters

These days, governance designations and certifications through sites such as our own, Professional Director (ProfessionalDirector.com), are also table stakes. Having your governance designation demonstrates that you have the essential governance skills needed to effectively lead and add value to the boardroom.

Serving on a board is very different from being an operational leader, manager, or executive. Your role is to oversee, ask great questions, and provide advice. It is not to operate the organization. This means you need to learn how to oversee at a different level than the CEO and executive team do. And it means you need to learn which aspect of the organization you must oversee. For example, a board should not be overseeing frontline staff. They should oversee the CEO. And they should oversee organizational human resources, philosophy, strategy, and culture. But the board is not the one to hire and fire employees. That should be left to the CEO and their team.

Governance matters. The better an organization is governed, the better the organization performs. The better a board member understands corporate governance and their role in it, the better they perform. Governance designations are no longer a nice-to-do. They are a need-to-do. They are table stakes. If you don't already have a governance designation, you should commit to getting one.

5. Diversity Matters

Today's boards are laser-focused on building a diverse team at the top. There is long-standing, significant research showing that a culture of equity, diversity, and inclusion (EDI) drives innovation, creativity, growth, and performance. It is both the right and the bright thing to do.

This is true not only for the rank and file but also in the boardroom. In the early days of EDI, organizations started with gender and then moved on to other visible diversity traits. Some continue to focus on "who" they are hiring. But many have moved on to ensure equity and inclusion are also priorities, so their diverse new hires have reason to stay. In other words, inclusion is more about the "what." By "what," we mean "What we can do to approach, support, encourage, and engage amid diversity?" Inclusion builds bridges to our commonalities and opens us up to relationships that allow us to build trust, respect, and healthy working environments and teams. This leads to better, wiser decision-making, which is a critical board-level skill.

The more you learn about diversity, the more you realize just how broad it is. What began as a fairly simple check-list of attributes—gender, geographic, heritage/culture, age, maybe one or two more—has morphed to encompass a broad range, including systemically under-represented groups such as Indigenous people, diversity of thought and learning styles, and invisible distinctions like neurodiversity.

The sheer number of dimensions that could potentially be identified and measured would practically overwhelm any board profile, along with a board application and subsequent vetting process. And if they include some diversity attributes, are they not unintentionally sending a message that other diversity attributes aren't important to them? Might an otherwise great candidate be turned off by the absence of their key attribute(s) and move on to the next opportunity?

Some organizations have responded by eliminating all references to specific diversity attributes. Instead, they ask applicants to self-disclose with an open-ended question like: "Tell us about yourself—what relevant aspects of your identity, lived experience, and diversity would you like us to know about and consider?"

This one question can open a door to a rich understanding of individuals' lived experiences and diversity that you could never get through even the most comprehensive applications and interviews.

There are a couple of downsides to this open self-disclosure approach, though. One is that the results are dependent on each individual's self-awareness and capacity (as well as willingness) to capture and share their relevant lived experience. Another is that it makes it very difficult for the recruiter to compare apples to apples and conduct any kind of systematic evaluation or benchmarking of diversity.

Instead, you can expect a "both-and" approach, at least for the foreseeable future. Organizations ought to continue to identify the top aspects of diversity that are important to them, where they seek value and have gaps, and include these in their board profile and application. They should be sure to cast the net wide—consider the broadest possible scope of diversity: visible and invisible, simple or complex. Plus, they should then add an open-ended self-disclosure question.

That way, a systematic identification and evaluation of specific diversity needs–like gender and geographic region, for example–can happen. Organizations can set diversity targets, measure their progress towards these, and achieve them. Research tells us that if you don't set targets and count numbers, equity, and diversity will never be achieved. You don't just get what you plan, after all; you get what you resource, what you measure, and what you reward.

And at the same time, organizations will benefit from rich learnings about candidates' lived experiences, and how that broad diversity might bring great value and insights to the board.

So, what are the implications to you as you seek to serve on a board?

First, you should include relevant aspects of your own diversity and lived experience in your Board-Ready Résumé. Don't limit yourself to the obvious ones; think long and hard about what you can bring to a board and organization. Just as you would for technical or industry expertise, research the company. What are their diversity needs, and which do you bring?

Second, be prepared to answer an open-ended self-disclosure question. These steps apply both to the initial application step and the subsequent interview step if you progress that far. Be ready with a great answer to the question, "What aspects of your lived experience and diversity would you like us to know about?"

Diversity matters. You will want to show a prospective board the ways in which you bring diversity to the team, whether that is visible or invisible diversity, and how you'll support an equitable and inclusive organization for all.

6. Attributes Matter

Personal attributes and competencies matter. Back in the day, when most board members were chosen because of who they knew, proving your competence was not a very high bar. Relationships remain an important part of getting board ready, but that will no longer be enough to garner you that coveted board seat you are hoping for. Board members will create a profile of the kind of expertise and perspective they need. They will compare your attributes to that profile. They will go as deep as probing your character traits. And, based on the gaps they have to fill on their profile, they will choose the candidate who best fills those gaps.

Attributes matter, and to be board ready, you need to clearly demonstrate why a board needs what you bring.

7. Words Matter

There are clues and hints within the wording of any board posting that point to the priorities they're seeking. What's more, the criteria are almost always listed in order of priority. Items near the bottom are attributes the board would like to have in a perfect world, but they are not as important as the criteria listed above them. For example, if a posting says, "Applicants MUST be financially literate," then you need to show that you can read financial statements of at least the same size, scope, and complexity of their organization's financial statements. Watch for the subtle differences in words like must, will, should, may, and prefer. These words matter, and you must be ready to address them.

Conclusion

When considering applying for a board seat, study the profile. And then study it again. Take note of specific attributes, skills, and experience that the board is looking for. Pull out that information and start to think about how you can fill in their gaps.

Remember: This isn't about what you need. When applying, the focus is providing boards with what they need. Once you have a thorough understanding of what their needs and gaps are, you can then start to craft your response and put together the perfect package that details why you're the right person for the job.

2

How to Network Your Way to the Boardroom

Many boards still use the "I know a guy" method of choosing directors, so networking is still needed, and visibility is a must.

—Dr. Debra L. Brown

Y ou probably didn't secure your current job by simply responding to a job advertisement, and it's highly unlikely you'll win a board seat by scanning postings too. Today's job searches, whether for hourly shift work, a C-suite position, or a board seat, are often all about networking online and in person. Teens get leads on first jobs from their network of friends and parents' friends. Professionals move up the ladder after years of building their own network of colleagues and, with the help of professional networkers, usually executive search firms with tentacles that reach even further.

In one 2023 CareerBuilder survey,[11] white-collar job hunters used both digital searches and personal networks in their hunt for new employment. Some 43 percent of white-collar respondents went to employer websites, and 30 percent took advantage of job boards during their search. But 39 percent also reported turning to friends and family, 28 percent noted job fairs where individuals can usually meet one-on-one with recruiters, and 22 percent said former colleagues were helpful. The hunt for a board seat isn't much different. In our experience, while posted opportunities can be helpful, they represent just a fraction of what's available. And, because those posted opportunities are publicly listed, they often are the most highly contested positions. If you are not using your contacts and building a network, your chances of getting the seat you want are extremely low. If you rely solely on responding to posted opportunities, you will not only have fewer opportunities, but you will also face much more competition for each opportunity.

Board members and human resources professionals are increasingly using their own networks and targeted searches through search and executive placement firms to find candidates. And they're more often relying on artificial intelligence tools to scour websites and social media platforms for candidates who fit their profile.

To get a board seat, today's candidates must move forward with a multi-pronged approach that includes not just scouring online listings and perfecting their board résumé. They also must build an authentic personal and professional network and fine-tune their brand and online presence. In this chapter, we cover how to put your best foot forward in this digital world.

The Power of Networking

Some people are collectors of connections. They can easily strike up conversations with strangers and aren't shy about reaching out to friends of friends, distant work colleagues, or college classmates they haven't chatted with in decades. Conversations with them are just easy—they flow. And these re-acquaintances are typically eager to reconnect.

For the rest of us, just the word *networking* conjures up feelings of forced interactions. And while we know we need to build and cultivate our network, it can just feel uncomfortable, even unnatural.

Regardless of where you fall on the spectrum, networking is a vital relationship-building skill that's key to securing any position—from employee to board seat. And, if you do it right, growing your connections will enhance your career—board and otherwise—immensely.

As you build your network, remember that you bring value to the relationship too. Just like in any great relationship, productive professional connections require a two-way street. Each party stays in it because they have a real interest in what the other person does and who they are. And, sure, you may want something from them, but they may also want something from you too in the future.

If networking makes you uneasy, the good news is that practice makes perfect. The more you network, the easier it will become over time. But the best networking strategy isn't haphazard. You are collecting valuable relationships. To do it right, you must cultivate your personal brand and then reach out to the right players. Here's how.

Cultivate Your Personal Brand

Networking is a sales job. And selling is serving. In this case, the product is you. Just like any good salesperson, you need to understand exactly what you're selling and how you will serve the organization and its board. And, when networking, what you're selling is your personal brand, or the unique experience, knowledge, and perspective you bring, along with how you can add value and serve others.

To cultivate your personal brand, conduct an honest and specific assessment of your experience. What skills have you developed over time, and what industries do you have experience in? Are there potential conflicts of interest, real or perceived? As you consider what you bring to the table, be sure to focus on what you can offer the board, not simply that you want a board seat. And, of course, manage your expectations. It's unlikely that your first board position will be with a Fortune 100 organization. Unless, of course, you are already uniquely prepared and equipped for the role.

Uncover the Influencers

Once you are clear on your personal brand, you can map out the right industries and companies to target in your networking efforts and uncover the influencers—board members and executives—who could be integral in your search. Here's the four-step process we recommend.

1. Assess the Companies

Find specific organizations in your target industry that you admire and study them. Understand and assess their strategy, financial health, leadership team, board members, approach to governance, and governance structure.

2. Rate Your Fit

Assess the company's board profile and compare your profile against their needs to determine whether you fill any of their gaps. These profiles are often in public documents that you can access from public disclosures on their website.

3. Find the Influencers

Now that you have a clear picture of each of your target companies and how you might best bring value, start building your connections. Who do you know? Is there a board member or senior leadership team member who may be a great connection in your search? If your target companies have a board-nominating committee, then those are the people, along with the CEO and board chair, who will likely be the most helpful to you.

4. Rinse and Repeat

As you make a list of several potential, specific, and targeted contacts, don't put all your eggs in one basket. Just be sure to prioritize your efforts to identify the best fit for your skills, experience, and passion, and keep hunting for great opportunities. Any connection you make, be sure to build on it. And be aware that unless you are an insider, it's often difficult to determine who holds the most sway over board selection. So just keep looking and asking.

So Easy! Right?

Now that you have your personal brand and list of targeted influencers in hand, you can get to work. Just pick up the phone! Send that email! Ask for that introduction! It's so easy! Or not. Let's be honest: Even if you have every tool and piece of knowledge at your disposal to link up with professionals who can move your career forward, introducing yourself to the right person at a networking event or even just clicking "Connect" on LinkedIn can be hard. Keep these tips in mind as you navigate those emotions and this journey.

- **Be Authentic**

Never put yourself out there as someone you're not. Just be yourself. Networking shouldn't feel false or contrived. As you manage your networking—in person and online—think about who you are as a person. How do you want to show that for people to see? How can you demonstrate that you're the right fit?

- **Watch For False Humility**

If you're an aviation expert, you don't want to go into a boardroom claiming to know only a little bit about the subject. But, in a room full of experts, you also don't want to come off as a know-it-all. False humility is not going to help you in this endeavor, and arrogance is as bad as underselling yourself. To develop the right tone, do an honest self-assessment. If you know a lot about aviation, say it, but then share your specific expertise and how you can add value.

- **Take, But Also Give**

If you want to build a network and create relationships that are strong enough to count on when you want that board seat, then you must be genuine. You have to take a real interest in others and make the other person feel as though they are important. If the relationship is all about you and what you get out of it, the other person will not feel valued, and the relationship will die on the vine.

- **Rekindle Relationships**

The easiest way to build your network quickly is by reaching out to people you already know, from past co-workers to customers to the parents you volunteered with at your child's school. These people know your strengths and weaknesses, and they know where you shine.

If you've lost touch, find a reason to reach out to them— maybe to celebrate an anniversary, promotion, or retirement— and then follow up to grow the relationship. As you reestablish the connection, make it about them. Take a sincere interest in them and offer something of yourself.

Because you already have a relationship, feel free to tell them you're interested in board work and ask their advice. If they're on a board, ask them how they got their seat. Have them review your board résumé for feedback. And offer to review theirs if they are on the same journey. While you start to rekindle and reaffirm those relationships, you can begin to work on developing new ones too.

- **Have Patience**

Networking is a long game, and the best time to establish a symbiotic relationship with someone is long before you need anything from them. If you haven't been a great networker in the past, it may take some time to reap its rewards, but the effort and patience are worth it. Networking is a bit like farming. You must plant your seeds in the spring before anything can grow and bear fruit at the end of the season.

Eight Steps to Effective Networking

1. Start with people you know, including referrals and contacts.
2. Build a relationship with those existing contacts.
3. Ask for introductions.
4. Ask someone to review your résumé.
5. Share your success stories with your contacts.
6. Follow up systematically with individuals.
7. Help them out.
8. Thank them.

Case Studies: Networking Superstars

As we're making clear in this chapter, if you want a really good paid board position, you'll most likely find it through networking, just like these professionals in our own network.

The Smart Networker

A woman landed five (that's 5!) significant paid board positions in a single year, and it all came purely through connecting with people she knew. What's more, she was so well-known and well-respected in her field that she didn't even have to interview for any of these positions. That's a lot of board opportunities being generated all through networking.

- **Lesson:** Networking is critical, and building a well-known and respected personal brand pays off in dividends.

The Friendly Flier

A recreational pilot spent a lot of time traveling for work. In his initial search for a board position, he targeted airport authorities and zeroed in on one, approaching them about a position.

They responded positively to his query and indicated they were interested in interviewing him, but then the pandemic hit. His search for a board seat was put on hold, but the organization told him to keep in touch. They assured him they would be interested in talking to him once aviation picked up again. And they did.

This is a terrific example of how the candidate reflected on what he likes, what he thought he could bring to the table, and the experience he had that he thought would be relevant to the organizations he researched. He put into practice everything we've been talking about. He was looking at it like a sales campaign, and the product he was selling was himself.

- **Lesson:** The best tactic is a targeted approach.

Growing Your Network

As you build a network with a future board seat in mind, trade groups and associations, executive search firms, and social media platforms play important roles in the journey.

As you network online, however, remember that those connections should grow more personal over time—moving from LinkedIn posts and likes to messages, emails, and in-person coffee meetups at association meetings and conferences.

- **Governance and Nominations Committee Members**

Who are the influencers in the organization you want to join? As an outsider, it is difficult to tell who exactly has the most influence on a board. Unless you're inside the organization, you can never know for sure, but there are some clues out there. If the board has a nominations committee or a governance and nominations committee, those committee members are in charge of finding new board members. Look to see who's sitting on those committees and who's chairing them. The committee and the board chair will probably have the best sense of what the board is searching for.

Remember the woman who had five opportunities offered to her without ever interviewing? Her situation may not be a typical example. You may still have to interview, but at least you'll find out about opportunities if you've networked with the right people—the CEO, the board chair, and the nominating committee. Don't rule out anyone else in the leadership team, though, or anyone else on the board. You never know who has the influence. There might be someone who's not on the nominations committee and who is not a chair but has the loudest voice in the room, who people listen to. Never turn down a networking opportunity at a target organization. Assess their board profile and determine whether you would fit and how your skills match up with what they need. Then, connect with them.

Board profiles usually exist for most organizations, often as public documents in one form or another. The whole profile may not be public, or the profile may be anonymized. But, often, they are included in a board's public disclosures on their website. These profiles usually describe the ideal board member and specify the skills and attributes that their board members must have. A lot of them even publish their matrix, so all the information you need is publicly available. This may not always be the case, but you'll find that if you really look, you can uncover what you need and then rate your fit with that board.

- **Groups and Associations**

Other ways to grow your network are joining groups, like social, alumni, service clubs, and church groups. You can also join a trade or industry association. These associations are organized groups where like-minded professionals join together. Associations can be local, regional, and even global in scale. These types of organizations also provide opportunities for getting a board seat. Typically, board members are elected from the membership of the association. On this type of board, you will need to build a network and run as a candidate for election to the board. Association boards can be very rewarding as you can contribute at the decision-making level of an organization important to you, with the larger associations providing compensation for your service.

- **Executive Search Firms**

To streamline the search process, boards are increasingly using targeted searches through executive placement firms to find board member candidates. Executive placement firms often have dozens of potential candidates at their fingertips. You, as a prospective board member candidate, can reach out to executive search firms directly. Usually, they have tools on their website where you can submit a résumé and even scroll through opportunities.

But it's important to remember that a board seat isn't a sure thing simply because you're working with an executive search firm—even with their connections and networks. Typically, when you connect with them, you're sending in an unspecific résumé, which doesn't always position you as the best fit for opportunities that pop up. Also be wary of any websites that ask you for payment to include you on a list of board or advisory opportunities. These could very well be scams.

Join an industry association to expand your network. The Institute of Corporate Directors (ICD) in Canada is one, as is the National Association of Corporate Directors (NACD) in the United States. Nonprofit, member-based associations also use search firms that match people with boards, or they might reach out to an industry association such as the ICD or NACD. When a suitable position opens up, they notify you. When those results come forward, absolutely reach out to them and let them know you're a good fit for a particular position.

- **Social Media**

From Facebook and Instagram to TikTok, X, and YouTube, the number of social media platforms is growing. But when it comes to professional networking, LinkedIn is king. According to Jobvite's 2020 Recruiter Nation Survey[12], the platform is the most popular social media channel for recruiting—72 percent of recruiters use it. In fact, HR tools are now designed to scrape publicly available information on LinkedIn profiles for specific criteria to uncover top candidates.

LinkedIn brings a bevy of benefits. It offers connections to a global network in every industry imaginable. Members totaled more than one billion across more than 200 countries and territories[13] in winter 2024, and they are all there for the same reason: to build business relationships.

It's also a kind of living résumé where your accomplishments and good work can unfold in real-time. You're no longer limited to that two-page résumé, which we'll cover in the next chapter. With each post, like, share, comment, and update on your LinkedIn page, you're building an up-to-the-minute résumé that anyone in the world can see.

What's more, LinkedIn offers a *who's who* inside organizations. When you go on an organization's website, you can find the names of board members and senior executives. With a quick online search, you can probably find these people's LinkedIn profiles and other social media handles. From there, you can dig into who they are, what their experiences are, and where you have commonalities. Maybe you attended the same university or launched your career at the same company years ago. Or, they may have connections to your connections. Once you start to network, you will find that the *five degrees of separation* idea is at play: You're probably only four or five contacts—maybe fewer—away from the president or the chair of your target board. You just have to spend the time making the connections.

But to get the most out of your LinkedIn page, you'll need to optimize your profile and boost your engagement on the platform to ensure the right people find you. Here's how to do that.

Fine-tune Your LinkedIn Profile

A LinkedIn profile includes far more than a typical résumé. Here are some key sections.

- **Perfect Your Description**

The description at the top of your LinkedIn profile isn't your job title. This is where you sell yourself. Use this description to capture people's attention and grow your connections. Include not only your title but also your accomplishments. Show your expertise right up front. In a sentence, explain who you are and what you do, working in keywords, if possible, which might make it easier for others to find you.

- **List Every Skill**

In the Skills section, LinkedIn lets you list fifty skills over three categories—industry knowledge, tools and technology, and interpersonal skills.[14] You may think that fifty skills are a lot. But it's likely, over the course of your career, that you've mastered that many or more. So, after an honest assessment of your accomplishments, fill in your fifty skills. Recruiters scan LinkedIn profiles for keywords and skills, so you'll have a better shot at rising to the top of their list if you've included the skills they're looking for.

- **Make It Public**

When you create or update your profile, make sure it is set to *public*. You want searchers to find you when they scour the site for people with the right skill set.

- **Keep It Professional**

Your LinkedIn profile will include a picture. Be sure to use a professional photo that shows your head and shoulders only—one that is clear and recent. Wear two things in your photo: business attire and a genuine smile.

- **Link Up on LinkedIn**

Once you've fine-tuned your LinkedIn profile, it's time to connect.

- **Expand Your Contacts**

If you haven't, start connecting with people you already have positive relationships with—past and present co-workers, old friends from college, neighbors, and friends.

Don't be shy about asking for connections from people you don't know. But, as you begin to connect with your target influencers, however, don't just hit "Connect." With every connection request, include a quick note to explain why you'd like to connect. It can be as simple as mentioning that you have a connection in common or that you enjoyed a recent article or video they shared. Be sure to let them know why you loved a specific piece of content and that you look forward to following them more closely. At this point, you are already asking to be connected, so don't ask for something more from them.

LinkedIn has a feature that lets you see who is looking at your profile. Take note. If they seem like a potentially valuable contact, send out a connection request if they haven't reached out to connect with you first.

Finally, remember that you are cultivating your personal brand, so don't accept all connections. You want to build connections that are perfect for your network.

• Be Active

Share, like, and comment on postings. Doing so takes little time, and being active raises your profile with the rest of your network and the extended network associated with those you have connected with.

And don't hesitate to share your own accomplishments. If you or your team won an award, share it on LinkedIn. If your company's LinkedIn page is celebrating a project that you worked on, share it with your network too.

• Share Your Thoughts

Your LinkedIn profile isn't just a glorified digital résumé. It's a place to share your expertise and thought leadership through posts, articles, and videos. Creating this kind of content takes more work. But, if it resonates with the right people, it can pay high dividends. Articles and video content can build your case as a leader in your field and allow you to reach a wide audience of business leaders.

Your articles and videos don't have to be long, but the content should be rooted in your experience so it is specific, relevant, and targeted. With each post, ask for feedback. As people share their own thoughts, be sure to engage with them, too. Again, networking is about building relationships. It is give and take, and engaging with meaningful, relevant content on LinkedIn is a great way to do both.

- **Find Your People**

Another way to connect is through professional LinkedIn groups. Alumni associations, trade organizations, and industry-specific professionals have created thousands of LinkedIn groups where like-minded individuals share tips, tricks, and, yes, job and board opportunities. We even have a group called Professional Director, where we share advertisements for board positions and other related information. If you ask to join that group, we'll add you.

If you want to further target your thought leadership, these industry groups provide a great way to engage in discussions about important topics in your field. There, you can build on your brand and establish yourself as a leader. It helps you find opportunities, and it helps opportunities find you. With each group you join, your LinkedIn feed will fill up with even more relevant content and connections that can vault you to the next phase of your professional life.

Rules of LinkedIn Engagement

In the busy day-to-day, things like building your professional presence on LinkedIn or any social media channel can fall by the wayside. You'll need to be intentional about making time to focus on it and be thoughtful in how you grow your brand there. Here's how:

Be strategic: Build your connections strategically and thoughtfully. While it may seem like a great idea to get as many connections as you can, over time, that approach will lead to significant "noise" on your LinkedIn feed and direct messages. Set goals for building your community on LinkedIn. Proactively target those types of connections that match those goals. For example, you may want to seek connections with governance professionals, serving board members, C-suite members, vice presidents, or director-level executives. Don't accept connections from individuals who do not match your sought-after profile. It's okay to say no to spammers.

Set a schedule: Make time each week—maybe 3 p.m. on Thursdays—to spend specifically on social media. Look to third-party tools to schedule posts to launch at a certain time. Learn the technology and use it so that your social media activity is not a burden on you.

Be social: Find out who's on the board you are interested in and ask yourself how you can be a hero to them. That can include liking and sharing their posts. When you share one of their posts, say something like, "This topic is something I've been thinking about a lot, and I really appreciate Alison's perspective on it. Check out her post and share it with your network. It's a great read." Don't forget to include their link. That way, you're helping your contacts build their networks while doing the same for yourself.

Keep it positive: It's highly likely that the recruiter for board positions or an organization's nominating committee will be looking at your social media footprint before they ever call you for an interview. Always keep your content current, positive, thoughtful, professional, and encouraging. This is not the place for content that makes fun of others. Politics and negativity are not appropriate. Your visual presence on LinkedIn is part of your image and brand, so make sure it reflects you in a positive light.

Grow your platform: Once you have mastered LinkedIn, use the articles, videos, and other content you have developed to leverage other social media sites. Keep your content on other social media sites clean as well, and stay positive. Being on a board puts you in the public eye. The bigger the organization, the bigger the lens. Treat all social media as business-friendly.

Conclusion

On this part of the journey to your board seat, you might be reminded a tiny bit of your childhood. All this networking is a little bit like making friends in the schoolyard. Some kids are comfortable running right into the center of it all; others are more comfortable on the sidelines.

The sidelines might have been fine in grade school, but prospective board members must be willing to run into the center and reach out. If you're the type who is less comfortable reaching out in person, networking online and starting to build relationships in the digital world may be easier. Your social media presence can be a great source of connections. And taking even incremental steps can move you closer to your desired destination—the boardroom.

As you begin to build your network, these tips can guide your way.

Narrow the opportunities. Look to the organizations where you can bring the most value and start connecting with board members and executives. Prioritize your efforts to where you see the most likely fit for your skills, experience, and passion.

Ask for referrals. Reach out to your contacts to find out if they know anyone on a board you are interested in joining. Don't be afraid to ask for an introduction.

Be responsive and helpful in return. Networking requires give and take. Thank your contacts when they give you something, and help them out when they need something in return.

Show an interest. When you're working a crowd, whether virtual or in-person, always make it a two-way conversation. Part of selling yourself is learning about them too.

3

The Perfect Match: How to Craft Your Board Résumé to Match What the Board Wants and Needs

You must craft a board résumé specifically for each opportunity.
And a board résumé differs from a résumé for a traditional job.

—Dr. Debra L. Brown

You probably have an executive résumé that's carefully crafted to fill the general needs of headhunters or potential employers as you look to step up in your career. It demonstrates your ability to lead with excellence and likely lists your academic and career history, the quantitative and qualitative results of your leadership, and how you fit within the hierarchy of the organization's leadership. That résumé is a starting point as you begin to apply for board seats, but it isn't enough to land you one. You need to craft your board résumé—your sales pitch—to the specific needs of the board.

After all, the first rule of résumé writing is to know your audience. And when you're working to win your first board seat, your audience and their needs are far different than a potential employer's. As we spelled out in Chapter 1, board members are keen to fill specific gaps in background and expertise when a seat opens up. There are plenty of subject matter experts who believe they're the right person for the job because, for example, they have experience running a company or deploying AI solutions across an organization. But, among all those experts, there are far fewer strategic thinkers and leaders. That's why your board résumé must demonstrate how you can rise beyond operations to corporate oversight and why you're the very best person to take that seat.

Your board résumé must answer how your particular insights will add value to the dialogue around the boardroom table and complement the team, not fit into some hierarchy. It must include not just your achievements but how you accomplished them. How did you lead and influence others? Because board members must also work collaboratively, your résumé must show how you're a team player too. And it must be customized for each and every seat that you apply for.

After all, each kind of board is seeking different skills. Candidate assessment criteria varies by the kind of board, whether it's a charity or a corporation. And it can differ by industry. The needs for a manufacturing company, for example, may be far different than a new tech startup.

And each board requires starkly different expertise. Boards with mostly white male members may be looking to diversify their ranks. Others may need experts in specific areas such as experience leading change management, running operations in Asia, or working in higher education.

The Four Rules of Board Applications

1. **Know your audience:** Determine the gaps that each board is keen to fill and customize your résumé to show how you will fill them.

2. **Illustrate your value:** Demonstrate how you will add value and new insights to the conversations and decisions for this particular board.

3. **Show your fit:** Explain how you complement the team, not how you fit into a hierarchy.

4. **Prove your successes:** Don't just say what you accomplished. Demonstrate *how* you achieved that success.

Your application package must show how you can and will bring a new and needed voice to the table. As you craft your board résumé, keep these tips in mind.

How to Structure Your Board Résumé

Unfortunately, there's no cookie cutter for board résumés. They don't need to look exactly the same as if they came out of some résumé mill. In fact, you don't want yours to look the same as someone else's. You want to stand out. But there are some essential pieces that every résumé should cover.

- **Name and Contact Information**

As with a regular executive résumé, put your name and contact information, including email, cell phone number, LinkedIn, and any other social media profiles, at the top. This helps interviewers quickly identify, retrieve, and catalog all the basic information they need before they even start scoring or evaluating the résumé.

- **Summary or Highlights Section**

Whether you call it the summary, highlights, or executive summary, this section should outline your unique story and why you're the best candidate for this particular seat. When board members read it, they should come away with a high-level view of who you are, what you've done, and where you've been.

Keep it brief: Limit it to just one or two paragraphs and tailor it to how you'll bring value to this particular board. Ensure it includes the key takeaways that you want board members to know about you and how you'll fill in the gaps on their board.

Make sure you can support it: You must be able to support the claims in your summary with the facts that come later in the résumé.

Get personal: Boards, these days, are looking for diversity in experience and perspectives. So don't just list data points; tell your story. If you bring diversity to the board, spell it out here. If you have strong character attributes that match the profile, introduce those here and weave them into the main content area of the résumé too. Remember, the reviewers might have hundreds of résumés to look at. Make sure yours gets a thorough review by catching their attention right away.

- **Experience**

If you have board experience, list that first in your board résumé. It's the most pertinent work experience that you'll bring to a new board. Make it easy for reviewers to find by putting it at the top of this section.

If you don't have board experience, never fear. Simply start with the experience that most closely aligns with other experiences they are looking for. For example, if they're looking for someone with human resources or education experience, don't make the reader dig through the résumé trying to find this vital piece of information; include it at the beginning.

In candidate profiles, boards list the most important skills first. Follow their lead. List the most important pieces first to show how you can fill their gaps. For example, if the organization is in the regional education sector and lists specific skills gaps in its ad as Financial Services Expertise, Client Engagement and Marketing Oversight Experience, and Human Resources and Talent Management Experience, then you might write something like this:

- Financial services expertise in areas including funds distribution, investment management, digital financial services offerings, low-cost investment options, and wealth management.

- Client engagement and marketing oversight experience across a spectrum of segmented groups in the virtual environment.

- Exposure to the regional education community with an appreciation for and understanding of the unique financial needs of the regional education workers and their families.

- Human resources and talent management experience at the strategic level necessary to chair the HR Committee.

On your board résumé, you'd want to list your financial services expertise first, followed by any experience in client engagement and marketing oversight, the regional education community, and HR and talent management.

- **Education and Affiliations**

Boards need curious lifelong learners, and the education section of your résumé provides you an opportunity to highlight that aspect of your life. Don't just list your MBA and governance certificates. Include all the courses you've completed and certifications you've received. If you are currently acquiring or interested in acquiring a designation, show it here, but also highlight it in your summary. You want the reviewer to see that you tick a bunch of boxes right away.

- **References**

References and endorsements will be required for just about any board candidate, and your research into a board's operations and needs can inform who you can ask to speak for you. For example, if the board seeks someone with human resources experience, you may want to find references who can speak to your expertise in that area. Meanwhile, if you find out that one of your contacts has deep ties to a current board member, ask for their endorsement.

Board Résumé Checklist

First Section: Your name and contact information.

Second Section: Tell your unique story in a short summary. Target it to the opportunity in front of you, highlight personal attributes, and ensure it's all supported by facts.

Third Section: If you have board experience, list it first. If you don't have board experience, list your expertise in the same order that the board has listed the desired skills in its candidate profile.

Fourth Section: Show your curiosity by including all learning and academic accomplishments. List any appropriate affiliations, such as Pro.Dir and specific industry certifications.

Best Practices

As you craft your résumé, keep these three points in mind.

• Keep It Short

When looking through long résumés, no one wants to dig through information we really don't care about. Reviewers often look over hundreds of résumés. If you haven't gotten a reviewer's attention by the first paragraph of a five- or six-page résumé, that's a problem for you and a red flag for the reviewer. They'll not only lose interest, but they'll also wonder whether you are an effective communicator—a key trait of any board member. After all, board members must be clear and concise and targeted in their language at the boardroom table. You'll need to make your case quickly and succinctly. If you can't be concise in writing on your résumé, the reviewer will conclude you won't be able to do so in the boardroom either.

Mark Twain is often quoted as saying, "I apologize for such a long letter. I didn't have time for a short one." Here's the rule of thumb: Just like any executive résumé, keep the entire résumé to no more than two pages. It must be concise and targeted to the opportunity. If you're having difficulty shortening it, consider taking something off the page that they haven't said they're looking for. Don't include your entire work history all the way back to your entry-level positions unless those experiences support your candidacy.

- **Share References at the Right Time**

It takes time to check references, and boards typically don't do it until after the first round. When they need your references, they'll let you know. And that's typically when you've been chosen for an interview.

Once it's time to share references, reviewers often are specific about what they want. They might ask for the names of three individuals and then contact one or all of them. Or they might ask for specific types of references—such as the chair of a board you sat on previously.

As you're picking the best references for you, you need to ensure that they will be honest about you and support your case for why you're the best person to fill the seat. They must be able to answer questions about your character and speak to those qualities that are hardest to convey from a résumé. After all, no matter how well a résumé is written, character attributes are difficult to portray.

During reference checks, reviewers aren't just verifying that you held a particular position or handled other administrative matters. They want to have a conversation with your references about who you are and will aim to validate what they heard from you in the interview to resolve any yellow flags that might have popped up.

- **Proofread. And Then Proofread Again.**

Always proofread your résumé! Better yet, have someone else proofread it for you. A fresh set of eyes is more likely to catch any errors. Having a clean, error-free résumé is part of putting your best foot forward.

I have literally reviewed thousands of résumés for job applicants over my career, and some of the simplest mistakes can stop you in your tracks. I reviewed a résumé recently for someone applying for a vice president's role. There was a three-year gap in the recent work history. Red flag or typo? In this case, it was a typo. However, this simple error can knock you out early in the process.

—Vicki Dickson, Senior Research Associate at Governance Solutions

How to Customize Your Board Résumé

When writing a board résumé, making strategic choices about what to reveal is crucial. Reviewers don't want to see extraneous information. They're looking for specifics in the résumé that demonstrate that you possess the skills, attributes, and qualities that they are looking for. Any information that doesn't relate to their candidate profile isn't important to them.

As we've spelled out, any board résumé must address *what's important to the board.* Here are some key steps to take as you fine-tune your board résumé.

Use the words and phrases in the candidate profile. If this terminology is missing from your résumé, add it in. It is critical that you incorporate their language into your résumé, or you will be screened out by commonly used hiring technology. For example, both Jobscan (Jobscan.co) and Resume Worded (ResumeWorded.com) will test the strength of your résumé against the posting.

Tell the story of why you're ready for board work. If you have a strong, successful career and now you want to become a board member for the first time, make sure your résumé demonstrates why you're ready for the role now. Highlight your career first and the achievements that will make you a great director for the target organization.

Share how you've helped boards in your previous employment or how you've collaborated or worked with boards. For instance, if you were a CFO, you were probably regularly supporting the board's audit committee and providing information to board members at meetings. Weave as much information into your story as you can about your association with any boards you have worked with to demonstrate that you understand how they govern.

Also include:

- Any training you've taken on governance or boards. Indicate your willingness to take the training if you haven't already done so.

- Applicable representational affiliations.

- Associated work or board activities that intersect with the candidate profile.

- Competencies based on the opportunity. A for-profit board will need people who can help with profit and revenue. A nonprofit board is seeking experts in fundraising and development.

List the right experiences if you have previous board experience. If you do bring a wealth of board experience, you don't need to list them all. If you've served on ten or more boards, omit the really small boards. Just include a statement saying, "Numerous not-for-profit boards to give back to my community," or specify the number of boards you have been on. However, if the candidate profile lists that diversity is important to the board, and your service on a particular board demonstrates your diversity or commitment to social justice, include it.

Best Practices

Here's how to handle two obstacles when seeking a board seat.

- **Conflict of Interest**

Conflicts of interest pop up from time to time when we're reviewing résumés. An elected municipal councilor, for example, may not be able to serve on a local corporate board if it does a lot of business with the town or city. Serving on the board of a competitor also will put you out of the running.

Other times, what might seem like a conflict of interest can actually serve as an asset. For the most part, boards are looking for people with experience on similar types of boards, often in the same industry. So, if you previously sat on the board of a competitor, you may be the perfect candidate for the other board now.

As reviewers weigh potential conflicts of interest, they'll be considering these questions:

- Can this candidate give us the best advice?

- Can they operate fully as a fiduciary for our organization?

- Are they members of a board with a competing interest?

Before you even apply, you should be asking these questions of yourself. And as you prepare for an interview, you should have your answers in hand.

- **Existing Commitments**

If you're currently sitting on four or five boards, a reviewer will wonder if you really have the time to commit to another organization. You will need to explain in some way how you have or will make time for all these commitments. Perhaps you don't have a full-time job. Maybe you're retired or a professional board member.

If you're about to term out on a board and are looking for a new opportunity, explain that on your résumé to ensure you're not leaving the reviewer wondering whether you can fully commit to their organization.

Top Three Traits for Board Members

1. **You are smart!** Now, some of the smartest people I know make some of the worst board members! The kind of smarts you need for serving on a board come from broad knowledge of business and strategy. You should be able to oversee what others do, ask phenomenal, thoughtful questions about their results, and then make quick decisions about what to do next. You don't need to be an expert in every area of business, but you do need to know enough to have turned your smarts into wisdom.

2. **You are experienced!** Boards are looking for people with experience. Full stop. If you don't have experience that is relevant to the board you want to join, then you are wasting your time and theirs. As referred to in Chapter 1, our course on how to get a board seat will tell you how

---

to know what any board is looking for and how to match the experience you have with what they need.

3. **You are focused!** What do I mean by that? I mean that you HAVE a focus! You have a particular skill set or industry focus that fits the company and the specific needs of the board. You are focused on the organization and its interests, not on yourself and your own interests. And you are focused on your role as a board member rather than trying to do management's job.

How to Demonstrate Your Unique Attributes

It's easy to list and prove objective metrics and facts—you held these five positions, increased sales by 100 percent, and reduced turnover by 50 percent. And it's easy to list certain personal attributes—that you're a team player with integrity, for example. But it's much more difficult to prove them.

These attributes, however, can be just as critical for boards as your specific skills and leadership experience. And, especially as boards look for diversity, demonstrating your specific background and perspective is critical.

Many times, if you've networked throughout your career, board members already are familiar with who you are and how you operate. Your reputation precedes you. And that's an important reminder to always be mindful of your actions and treatment of others.

You also can demonstrate who you are through your affiliations. Do you volunteer with a local nonprofit? Do you give back through professional organizations? Are you a longtime mentor or sponsor of others? These can be experiences to mention in your board application.

Board interviews, which we'll cover more deeply in the next chapter, provide an opportunity to demonstrate your unique abilities and character as well. Be ready to answer open-ended questions about your traits, such as:

- Tell me about a time you handled conflict.

- What motivates you?

- How would your colleagues describe you?

- What are the key strengths that you would contribute to the board's performance?

- Describe a major initiative that you have been involved in as a board member. What was your role, and what did you accomplish?

- What steps have you taken to be an effective board member and stay up to date on these good governance practices?

Your references should also be able to speak to your character, not just your leadership abilities. So, be thoughtful about who you select.

And, of course, the cover letter is another opportunity to demonstrate who you are and why you don't just have the skills but the right attitude for a board seat.

Sometimes, people wonder if they should include a photo in their application. This is always a plus. If you're a visibly diverse candidate, a photo may be particularly helpful. However, if you do plan to use a photo, be careful about what kind of photo you use. Whether you hire a professional photographer or have a friend snap the picture, make sure it's professional. Wear business attire and ensure there isn't a lot of clutter in the background.

A Word on Cover Letters

Your résumé is about you. Your cover letter must show the reviewer that you understand their organization, you've done your research, and you have a compelling reason to want to be on their board.

It can include some of your story to illustrate how your experience can fill the board's gaps and add value to it. It also should indicate why you want to be on the board other than getting paid or being eager for the title. In the cover letter, you must show that you have some connection to and passion for the organization.

Of course, reviewers also know that a great cover letter doesn't necessarily indicate a great applicant. Anyone can hire a service to write a great cover letter. During the initial review stage, reviewers will be focused primarily on your résumé to ensure you have the key skills they are looking for. Use your cover letter to supplement those *what* and *how* details in the résumé with the reason you want to fill the role and why are the right person to do it.

Conclusion

With these first three chapters, you have the tools to begin to map out your own plan and set goals tailored to your specific situation.

You know how to identify what board members need as they seek to fill open board seats, as covered in Chapter 1. You know how to build your own network of contacts who can help you on your path to a board seat, as covered in Chapter 2. And you're familiar with best practices as you set yourself up for success and craft the perfect résumé, as we covered in this chapter. The next stop is the interview, and how to ace that is exactly what we'll cover in Chapter 4.

Example Résumé

Stuart Almond, MBA, Pro.Dir®
Address
Cell: 000-000-0000
example-email@example.com

Summary

Experienced Board Member with significant leadership and pension benefits experience. Have been the Chair of the Board and chaired human resources committees on several boards, including during benefits and pension transition and implementation initiatives. **As the son of a Moroccan mother and English Father, I bring a diverse perspective to the boards I serve on. As the husband and brother of teachers, I value, understand, and support the work of Teacher's Financial.** Thorough understanding of fund management and oversight at both the executive and board level. Exemplify the character traits of integrity, curiosity, and teamwork. Greatly value the work and welfare of teachers and support them in receiving the financial services they deserve.

Skill Areas

Pension Governance	Human Resources Oversight
Risk Direction and Oversight	Strategic Planning
Financial Literacy	Process Improvement
Governance Expertise	Team Leadership

Board Experience

Director, ABC Corp.   2017 – Current   **Chair Governance Committee, Member HR Committee**

ABC Corp. is a billion-dollar US-based agri-business, supplying cutting edge automation equipment to the worldwide dairy industry. The board oversees a billion-dollar defined benefit pension.

Lead Director DEF Corp   2014 – 2020   **Lead Director**

DEF Corp is a family-owned automotive parts supplier that operates throughout North America with revenues approaching $750 million. The board oversees a defined contribution pension plan.

Chair, GHI Corp.   2012 – 2020   **Chair HR Committee, Governance Committee, Board Chair**

GHI Corp is a multi-billion-dollar robotics company that provides automated welding and assembly robotics to OEMs in the automotive and farm implement sectors. The board engineered a successful transition from a defined benefit plan to a defined contribution plan.

Chair MyNFP   2001 - 2013   **Chair Finance, HR, and Governance Committees, Board Chair**

MYNFP is a charitable corporation that provides the gift of water to remote areas and communities in sub-Saharan Africa.

Director, MyCorp   1996 – 2016   **CEO/Director**

MyCorp is a $250 million dollar farm implement widget provider.

Director MyHealth   1995 – 2000   **Director, Audit Committee, Governance Committee**

MyHealth is a Hospital foundation that contributes 10 million dollars annually to the local Hospital's Capital programs.

Director YouthSport   1994 -1998   **Director, HR Committee**

Youth Sport is an integrated, registered local charity that fundraises and supports local sports programs and facilities, raising and distributing over $1 million annually.

Professional Experience

Chief Executive Officer: NewCorp Inc., Anytown   **2017 to Present**

Leader of a ~$100 million custom agricultural manufacturing company focused on providing cost-effective crop drying and storage solutions.

Accomplishments:

Creating and leading a world-class, diverse team is my greatest accomplishment. Have grown and implemented innovative strategies that have propelled NewCorp from a small regional player to a ~$100-million-dollar, profitable business in just 7 years.

	Revenue	Gross Profit	Employees	Employee Benefits	Employee Pension
2017	$1.1 million	$ 75,000	6	None when purchased company	None
2024	$100 million	$ 19 million	350	All employees: medical, dental, vision	Defined Contribution

Founder and Chief Executive Officer: MyCorp Inc., Sometown
1996 -2016

Founded, led, and built a farm implement manufacturing company from a one-person shop into a ~$250 million international supplier of farm widgets on three continents. Responsible for manufacturing facilities in Canada, Poland, and China.

Accomplishments:		Revenue	Gross Profit	Benefits
	1996	$50,000	$ 0	None
Education	2016	$250 million	$ 64 million	Medical, Dental, Vision, Defined Contribution Pension

Pro.Dir Certification	Professional Director	2018
MBA	University of Toronto	2011 – 2013
Bachelor of Commerce	McMaster University	1991 – 1995

Other Certificates and Courses

Financial Literacy for Board Members, Human Resource Oversight Certificate, Cyber Security Risk Oversight, Strategy Development, Enterprise Risk for Boards of Directors, Quality Leader for Six Sigma, Coaching Level 3, LEAN 6 Sigma Black Belt certified.

Affiliations

Member of Institute of Corporate Directors, Professional Director, Educators Technology Association

4

How To Ace the Interview

To ace any interview, don't fly by the seat of your pants! You must do your homework.

—Rob DeRooy

Through the years, we've interviewed dozens of board candidates, and one of our favorite questions to ask remains this: "How did you prepare for today?" We often follow that question up with two more: "What is one thing that jumped out at you from this research?" and "What challenges do you see ahead of us?"

These aren't trick questions. We ask candidates at every level to answer them. We do it because we want to see how committed the applicant is to this recruitment process and how committed they are to the role. Are they interested in a board seat to pad their résumé and earn a little extra money? Or are they in it because they have a genuine interest in supporting the organization and sharing their expertise and perspective?

Reaching the interview stage for an open board seat is something to celebrate on its own. Just a fraction of applicants typically make it this far, and the final candidates are often equally qualified for the role. How well you do in the interview can make or break your candidacy. We've seen too many qualified candidates come in for interviews and be immediately disqualified because they were unprepared. In other words, when you reach the interview process, know that every stage of your career has led you to this moment. Your performance must be flawless. You'll need to deliver the right answers, ask on-point questions, and come prepared with relevant anecdotes and responses.

This, of course, is all easier said than done. Not everybody looks forward to a job interview. According to one survey by JDP, an employment screening firm,[15] some 93 percent of U.S. workers have experienced job interview-related anxiety. Being unable to answer a difficult question, looking nervous, and not coming off as intended are the top three stressors, according to the survey.

But there's a proven way to combat those rattled nerves, ease the anxiety, and execute an impeccable performance: Prepare.

In this book, we've revealed in Chapter 1 how to decipher what boards really want. In Chapter 2, we've covered why networking is so important. And, in Chapter 3, we've shared the secrets to crafting a board résumé that meets an organization's specific needs.

Now, it's time to ace the final step—the interview. In this chapter, we'll share a step-by-step guide for how to research opportunities, what to consider as you do all that homework, and how to talk about yourself and put your best foot forward.

Gather the Research

If you've spent your career in a particular industry, you may go into an interview for a board seat with plenty of knowledge about the sector and the organization. But, as we've written before, boards aren't just looking for long-time leaders in their specific field. In some cases, they need outsiders who bring relevant experience to the table—leading a digital transformation, expanding into Asia, or representing a more diverse perspective. In either case, general knowledge about a company or industry—gleaned from business news headlines or from working in the industry but not with the organization—isn't enough.

Winning candidates for board seats must demonstrate they understand the organization's business model and the challenges and opportunities in the industry. And they can't just come in with the facts. They need to showcase that they've developed opinions and ideas about what steps and strategies can drive the business forward into the future.

Focused research of the industry and the company is key. Thankfully, social media, organization websites, trade publications, legal filings, and other easily accessible data online provide plenty of information for your in-depth look.

As you research, remember this: While your hunt for a board seat is often very similar to a job search, the role is quite different. Your research should be about more than simply knowing some information about the industry, it should be about knowing the industry well enough to be able to talk about its issues and winning strategies. Your goal is to be seen as a *peer*, not a candidate.

Here are some of the key pieces of information that you should familiarize yourself with to ensure you can demonstrate that you know the industry inside and out.

1. Annual Reports

While these likely won't be available for private companies, public companies, government agencies, and nonprofits, all publish reports that sum up their work in the past year and provide some insights about what's to come.

For public companies, in particular, the management discussion and analysis, or MD&A, can be particularly insightful. In MD&As, management, typically in an easy-to-understand narrative form, lists an organization's key risks and the mitigation strategies that they use to address them, macroeconomic pressures, future plans, and new projects. They provide great information about an organization's business model and strategies.

The annual report for a nonprofit covers what it has accomplished and should include information about its revenue and expenses, major donors, and the success of initiatives and plans for new ones.

Government agencies also publish annual reports that include an MD&A, financial statement, and audit reports, among other data.

2. Board Member Bios

You may already know who is on the board through your professional network. If you don't, corporate websites or annual reports often list them. Once you have the names, you can do more thorough research on them, finding their LinkedIn page and searching for their professional accomplishments.

Look for shared experiences or colleagues. Did you attend the same college? Did you launch your career at the same consulting firm? Were you speakers at the same conference a few years apart? As we covered in Chapter 2, shared backstories can help as you seek to build your network.

3. Corporate Website

Click beyond the home page, and you may find a treasure trove of information about how the business operates. Here's what to look for:

- **Strategic plan:** Even if it provides a broad-brush, high-level look, you may be able to glean a few insights from the document.

- **Mission, values, and culture:** This should explain the why behind what the organization does—whether it's making sandwiches or selling software—and how its people operate to accomplish that mission. For example, does the company operate with a hard-driving culture of innovation and achievement, or is it more focused on formal rules and stability?

As companies interview you for a board seat, it's likely they'll be considering whether you are the right culture fit for them. And as you do your own research, you should ask the same question of yourself. If you're a leader who embraces innovation and an entrepreneurial spirit, you may not want to help lead a buttoned-up company that thrives on rule-following.

- **ESG reports:** Thanks to expectations from investors, consumers, and employees, a growing number of public and private companies are publishing ESG, or environmental, social, and governance, reports. These reports highlight how companies operate, including initiatives that aim to protect the environment, social programs that ensure employees are treated fairly, and governance practices that make certain leaders and employees operate ethically.

4. Social Media

Follow the organization's social media accounts and take note of the kinds of content they are promoting. What employee stories and successes are they sharing? What other organizations are they collaborating with? How do they present themselves to the public—in a conservative manner or in a light-hearted, fun-loving tone? Does it match your own style or belief system, or is it contrary to how you operate in the world?

5. Business Headlines

Spend some time pouring over news covering the industry to look for emerging trends and challenges, statements from leaders and board members, and what the organization's competitors are doing.

6. Competitor Websites

While you're googling, get to know the organization's competitors too. What are their risks and mitigation strategies? How well are they following through on their ESG priorities? How are they addressing the future? Your knowledge of competitors can demonstrate an understanding of the industry and can provide fodder for interview questions that focus on how you might respond to market forces.

7. Governance Ratings

Professional rating agencies are increasingly evaluating the management of companies and provide some accountability for board and corporate operations. They offer insights into how well companies are conducting business compared to their peers and any potential room for improvement.

Do Your Homework

There are two reasons you need to do this research. First, you need to be prepared for the questions they'll ask you during an interview. Second, you'll need to be ready to ask important and interesting questions of the people who are interviewing you.

If you've done your research, when they ask you why you want to be on a board or what you know about the organization, you can give thoughtful responses. If they don't ask you those penetrating questions, you can pose thoughtful queries to them that show your depth of knowledge and interest and make you more appealing as a candidate.

That's why, as you gather your research, you'll need to read it all with a critical eye as you think about how your own expertise and perspective can help the board oversee how the organization responds to risks, shores up revenue, or launches new plans and projects. As you read through everything you've gathered, think about questions like these: Did you navigate a similar risk in a previous position? Do you have deep experience in a sector they're interested in moving into, for example, a software company that serves higher education clients and is now venturing into nonprofits too? Are their competitors beating them in a particular offering that you've been successful with?

And don't just read the information; analyze it. **As always, remember this:** You are not interviewing with people who will be your bosses. You're interviewing for a board seat with potential peers who will want to take advantage of your expertise and experience. They expect that you'll come up with opinions about business operations, growth strategies, your governance role, and other needs.

Of course, as an outsider, you may not fully understand their strategy and risks. Especially with private companies, you may be able to find little more than general information about their operations. That's okay. The board knows whether information about their company is freely available. They expect you to come to the interview with a perspective or opinion—not an edict. Don't be afraid to tell them, "From my research, I think that probably the key risks for the industry and your organization are in this area." Make sure they understand that you've got a perspective on the risks but that you also recognize that you may be wrong. Don't purport to be the expert from a little extra research.

You do, however, want to make sure they understand that you've done the work and have some insights into what they're going through. The better your research, the richer those insights will be.

Sell Yourself

As you research and analyze your findings, keep in mind the kinds of questions that interviewers will ask. They typically come in two forms: the standard who, what, when, where, and why questions about your skills and experience and more open-ended behavioral questions that are designed to shed light on how you behave and work with others.

A common standard question is, "Why do you want to be on our board?" The right answer to that question will be based on your knowledge of the industry and organization and how your knowledge intersects with their needs. Your response shouldn't focus on what you'll learn from being in the boardroom but on what you can bring to the board.

Another standard question is, "What do you know about this industry?" This is an opportunity for you to really shine. If you've done the right homework, you know what the major risks and opportunities are, and you can speak to the company's strategic approach to addressing the risks and optimizing the opportunities.

Behavioral questions usually start with a phrase such as, "Tell me about a time." They beg for a great story, and you will greatly benefit if you have some anecdotes and examples ready. Your stories could focus on showing your skills, but interviewers will more likely want to hear stories that demonstrate your character attributes, such as ethical behavior, teamwork, and leadership abilities. These traits are difficult to demonstrate on a résumé, so they are often tested during the interview.

For example:

"One of my attributes would be that I am non-judgmental. I will always listen to both sides of any issue. I am fair and unbiased, so I come to any situation with no preconceived notions. I am understanding, kind, and compassionate, but I am never afraid to make a decision, even if it would make me unpopular. A position on the board is not a popularity contest, but a way to protect the organization and effectively govern."

"Listening to the conversation is important; knowing when to ask open-ended questions that allow us to clarify or learn more is a skill that I use daily. In my role, I am asked to make critical decisions. My approach is to listen and ensure I have all the information and am aware of my body language and verbal tone. Practicing non-judgmental listening by setting aside my own biases or points of view is a skill that I have learned."

The art of nailing the interview comes down to two things. You must do a great job promoting yourself, which doesn't come naturally to everybody. And you need to tell some great stories, especially if an interviewer uses behavioral interview questions, which they most likely will. Show them how you uniquely match their desired profile. The good news is that even an anxious interviewee can rise to the top of the candidate list with the right preparation, mindset, planning, and a great story. While it's unlikely you'll have an immediate answer ready for every question they'll ask, here's how to anticipate the most likely queries and come prepared for anything.

1. Brand Yourself

Your brand is a true expression of your character strengths and skills, what's important to you, and how you lead. It must be honest and accurate to you—and, most importantly, feel and be authentic. If you're a quiet, thoughtful leader, don't try to sell yourself as somebody who is brash and hard-charging. As you prepare for your interview, think deeply about who you are and how you lead—what your brand is.

If you're not used to blaring your successes, it might feel uncomfortable to even talk about having a personal brand. But who you are and what you bring—your brand—will inform how you answer interview questions, especially behavioral queries. If you're a collaborative leader, and the question is about how you lead, your answer should demonstrate how you work with others to make big decisions. If you have had great success leading companies through difficult times, your answers will reflect that can-do spirit. Be ready to own your brand and be boastful—even if, on brand, it's in your naturally quiet and thoughtful way. In this case, false modesty is not your friend.

2. Consider the Candidate Profile

In Chapter 3, we covered the importance of using the candidate profile to customize your board résumé. As you prepare for the interview, the board member profile can provide plenty of clues about the kinds of questions interviewers may ask you. As you get ready, the answers to these three questions can help you look more critically at the profile and get ready for the queries that might be posed. Based on the profile:

1. What skills, experience, and knowledge could be tested in the interview?

2. What behavioral-based interview questions might the interviewer ask?

3. What are other, more standard interview questions that you predict will be asked?

If you see that they're looking for certain skills, prepare an anecdote that would show your knowledge in those areas or, better yet, a story that shows them you can use those skills in a board setting.

For example:

"I always challenge myself to be a good listener. I like to clarify at the beginning of a conversation what the topic is and establish my role as just a listener. I won't offer comments or suggestions. I listen to know how best to interject. Depending on who initiated the conversation, I let them present the facts, don't interrupt, and refrain from offering input if it's not expected or wanted. Once the facts are presented, if expected, I simply paraphrase what was said, ask any questions to clarify information, and then make comments.

"Throughout my career in mental health and addiction treatment, I have been able to develop expert professional judgment and critical-thinking skills. I perform very well under high-stakes and unpredictable environments, which has allowed me the confidence to navigate critical thinking in any situation. In my experience as a crisis responder, I have had to be in situations that require me to be constantly assessing the environment I am in, processing high volumes of information from various outputs, and being confident in my ability to make consecutive decisions based on my observations and evaluation of information being presented to me. Decisions that I make always consider the impacts with great care and attention to all involved. From working and leading in such high-stress situations, I have been able to adapt and appreciate honing and focusing on those skills. It's allowed me to better ensure that the right decisions are made, considering all outcomes, intentions, and impacts."

3. Curate Your Stories

As you think about your own personal brand and the candidate profile, you'll want to come to the interview prepared with an inventory of 10 to 20 stories that exhibit your skills, character, and personality traits that are uniquely you.

You might have to dig deep to find all the successes you have had along the way and all the stories that explain who you are, how you lead, and what is important to you. It will take time to develop a depth of stories, but it is time well spent. Once you have developed those stories, you can pull them out whenever you need them.

Make sure your stories are based on real-life experiences that show how you contribute, lead, and act. The better your stories and the more practiced you are at telling them, the better your interviews will be.

Story Building Tip: Be A STAR

If you're having difficulty building your stories, keep the **STAR** acronym in mind. STAR stands for Situation, Task, Actions, and Results. With each story, begin by explaining a specific *situation* and *task*. Then, spell out the *action* you took in that situation, followed by the *results* that were achieved because of your actions. As much as possible, the results should be specific and measurable.

Consider this example.

Situation: An organization's entry-level employees were diverse. But as workers moved up into management, the ranks grew less diverse.

Task: To build a more equitable and inclusive workforce that retains diverse employees and helps them move into more senior roles.

Action: Developed internal mentorship and employee sponsorship programs, launched employee networking groups and offered new continuing education programs designed to provide junior-level employees with management skills.

Results: Within five years, management and executive-level teams were 25 percent more diverse.

Warning: Speed Bumps Ahead

In board interviews, these three obstacles and issues are common—and easily surmountable.

- **No Board Experience? No Worries**

During an interview for a board seat, your stories and anecdotes should include your experiences serving on other boards. But what if you don't have much board experience—or have never served on a board before? Never fear. Nobody comes out of the womb as a board member. Every board member once interviewed for their first boardroom seat. And especially if a board is seeking to diversify their roster with people from varied backgrounds, they may expect candidates to not have previous board experience.

If you don't have much board experience, build your stories around experiences from your previous management and leadership positions. Think about times when, perhaps, as an executive, you interacted with your organization's board. Make sure your stories demonstrate the journey you've taken so far to become a successful leader.

- **Don't Just Be a Leader**

Plenty of boards are full of really great CEOs, but really great CEOs don't necessarily make great board members. That's because some CEOs are used to being *the* leader rather than one of many. Group decision-making can sometimes be difficult for these people, especially if they're a *follow-me* kind of leader. But on a board full of leaders, taking the *follow-me* approach can be counterproductive. Boards really need members who can work together to make decisions. Make sure your stories demonstrate how you can partner and collaborate.

- **Listen and Stay on Message**

During any interview, the worst thing you can do is give an answer that's unrelated to the question. For example, a colleague once sat through an interview where the prospective board member got nearly every question wrong. He wasn't listening. Instead, he'd come to the interview with stories to tell, and he told them regardless of what he was asked. It was a disaster. It's vital to listen to the question and make sure you answer the question posed.

If you aren't 100 percent sure what you're being asked, clarify the question before you answer to make sure you understand what the interviewer is looking for. You don't want to ramble. Don't be afraid to ask for clarity to avoid answering the wrong question. When the interviewer asks an open-ended question such as, "Tell me about a time you went above and beyond," don't be afraid to clarify, "Would you like a professional example or a personal example?" and let them choose. Have your answer ready on both accounts. Asking for clarification shows respect and demonstrates that you're listening carefully to their questions.

Proven Interview Tips

In addition to doing solid preparation before the interview, here are some other common-sense tips.

Dress the part: Groom impeccably. Avoid using scents. Especially if the interviewer has allergies or sensitivities, a heavy scent will be off-putting.

Check your settings: If the interview will take place online, ensure you have a good internet connection and keep your background neutral. Political, offensive, or otherwise inappropriate items in the background will be off-putting. Clutter also may count against you. Arrive early. And finally, make sure there will be no interruptions. Keep pets in a different room and prep children and others in the house ahead of time so that they know you are not to be interrupted during the time of the interview.

Practice, practice, practice: Interviewing well is a skill that needs to be kept sharp. Find somebody—a family member, friend, or colleague—who you can practice your interview skills in person, by phone, or online. Practice sharpens the message and keeps you from becoming a rambler.

Be ready for a crowd: Unless they've hired a search firm, boards often conduct panel interviews. Members of the board's governance committee or governance and nominating committee are usually going to be involved in the interview. Every person in the interview will have a set of questions. So that they're fair to all the candidates, interviewers typically ask every interviewee the same questions.

Write it down: After leaving an interview, immediately write down as many of their questions as you can recall and note which story or example you used. Then, the next time you interview, you can pull out your storytelling playbook and refresh and improve upon your answers. Over the years, you will build an excellent compilation of all the best and worst questions and answers. Writing them down helps you keep a record of them and also ensures you can recall them easily and quickly for the next interview.

Use your manners: Regardless of whether the interview was in person or through video, follow up with a thank-you note. You may or may not get the board position, but if you got as far as the interview and ultimately weren't chosen, you at least know you were a strong contender. The reviewers and interviewers spent a great deal of time looking at your application, researching you, and interviewing you. As old-fashioned as it may seem to some, sending a thank-you note, likely through email, is still best practice. It shows your appreciation for their consideration and for the time they took to seriously evaluate your fit for the board.

Analysis: Potential Questions

There are some typical questions a potential board member can anticipate being asked. Each query is followed by suggestions on themes and ideas to include when answering these questions.

Skills and Experience Questions

In the profile, the board spells out its desired core skills in the following bullet points, which provide some insight into what the focus of their queries will be.

- The board seeks to be diverse, inclusive, and reflective of the education community that we serve.

- The board seeks someone with a depth of executive-level management experience, including strategic planning, risk management and oversight, human resources, and technology oversight.

Here are some potential questions.

1. What is the role of the board of directors?

Answer: Show that you understand best practices in board governance, the board/management relationship, director responsibilities, and fiduciary duties. Candidates also may need to demonstrate an understanding of how the role of the board of directors is different from executive-level and C-suite management and what makes for an effective board member.

"The primary role of the board is to be responsible for the corporate governance system of the organization. That means the system of direction and control. The board sets the strategic direction of the organization, puts in place its leadership, and then monitors actual performance to gain confidence that we're heading in the right direction. It delegates day-to-day operations to management through the CEO."

2. Briefly describe to us your board experience.

Answer: Share any board experience in corporate or non-profit organizations, including board or committee leadership roles.

"I was invited to serve on my first board when I was 17 and haven't stopped since! I concentrate on serving on one or, at the most, two boards of complex organizations because of the time commitment, and then also a smaller not-for-profit board to give back to the community. Because of my financial and accounting background, I almost always serve on the audit committee, although I enjoy serving on and even chairing the governance committee from time to time."

3. How financially literate are you? How did you gain that knowledge?

Answer: Provide your Pro.Dir designation or equivalent and explain how you gained your financial literacy.

"I would describe myself as strong in terms of financial literacy, more than competent but just a little short of expert. Most of my financial accounting expertise was gained while serving as a financial executive and then a chief executive, as well as having earned my Pro.Dir designation. So, I have a strong familiarity with how to read financial statements, especially understanding their linkage to strategy and the business model. With my background in risk management, I am also strong at using financials to recognize red flags, indicating potential business risks."

4. Tell us about your depth of expertise in our industry.

Answer: Demonstrate your experience in challenging industry trends and, more recently, in technological advances.

"I have spent much of my professional career working in the broad financial services industry. I have worked in the head office of one of the largest banks in the country in operations and business development. Further, I worked in branches and commercial centers in commercial lending and institutional banking. In those roles, I was responsible for business development and sales. All these experiences give me a strong background that's beneficial and applicable to the insurance business, particularly in risk management and business development strategy. I see and understand emerging risks and opportunities in your business, beginning with a digital strategy and capitalizing on technology like AI while mitigating cybersecurity risks. AI and digital marketing, including on social media, are the future of sales and business development for any retail business. My experience would add to the board's capacity and strengths in these areas."

5. What are the unique financial needs of workers in this organization or industry?

Answer: Show your exposure to the organization and industry's community with an appreciation for and understanding of the unique financial needs of the workers and their families.

"The hospitality industry has traditionally attracted entry-level workers and not paid them very well. One of the keys to attracting and retaining the best employees is to "walk the talk" when it comes to a healthy workplace culture, flexible workplace and hours, and a broad range of benefits that include caring for employees' mental and physical health. These can help to offset a traditionally low-wage industry and position the best employers well. Walking the talk also means aggressively ensuring equity, diversity, and inclusion. This again is especially important in an industry which traditionally draws workers from marginalized and diverse groups."

6. Tell us about your experience with HR oversight.

Answer: Demonstrate your human resources and talent management experience at the strategic level necessary to chair a board's HR committee.

"Having spent my entire career moving up the management ranks of large firms, I have direct experience in managing large, diverse, and complex teams and everything that requires. Having served both on boards and as a C-suite level executive, I understand the difference between human resources oversight and human resources management. I am thoroughly familiar with HR oversight tools like balanced scorecards, employee engagement, and other EDI metrics, strategies, and monitoring tools. An HR committee's role is to provide independent oversight to the broad direction of human resource strategy, including executive compensation, but I would say particularly organizational culture. Of course, it's up to the CEO to manage day-to-day HR issues and hire and fire individuals. But the committee must monitor employee engagement tools and other strategies to ensure they remain confident in the CEO's workforce management approaches. It's a fine line, but with experience and when done right, a board's HR committee can really add great value to the organization that's appreciated, and not resented, by the CEO."

7. Tell us about your experience with strategic planning.

Answer: Share any strategic planning experience at the board level or with a board to demonstrate that you understand the board's unique role in this process.

"As a CEO and long-time C-suite executive, I've been closely involved in the development of numerous multi-year strategic plans, which were created in collaboration with the board, staff, and stakeholders. I have a strong grasp on the strategic thinking and planning process, from stakeholder engagement through town halls, focus groups, and social media to e-scans and i-scans, including SWOT analysis and scenario planning. I have facilitated joint board-staff strategic planning sessions where we converge on the right vision, mission, values, and goals. And we don't stop until we have a clear set of 'SMART' objectives in place for management to achieve and the board to monitor. I've found that strategic planning is so much more than an event; it's a process that calls for preparation, patience, and perseverance, as well as clarity of leadership and consensus-building."

8. Tell us about your experience with risk management and oversight.

Answer: Showcase any risk management and oversight experience at the level necessary to lead the organization through risks and challenges.

"While 'risk management' can mean many things to many people, at the board level, I like to frame this through the lens of the strategic plan and risk oversight. Risks and opportunities are uncertainties that can either keep you from achieving your strategic objectives or make it easier to reach them. By framing risk tolerances (acceptable levels of risk) and risk appetite (desirable levels of risk) in the language of strategic priorities and performance measures, risk management is integrated with strategic planning and, therefore, with performance and risk oversight. A couple of other thoughts come to mind here. Risks can helpfully be organized by goal and objective area (for example, HR risks, financial risks, IT risks), and a further categorization as 'known' and 'unknown' risks. Known risks are usually susceptible to quantification and periodic reporting in an ERM system, but unknown risks call for real-time reporting and mitigation. Like most areas affecting the board, it's important to draw a line between the board's role in risk oversight and management's role in risk management."

9. What does it mean to you for a board to be *strategic*?

Answer: Provide a specific example of how the board might get involved in corporate strategy without getting into operational details and activities.

"When I hear 'strategic,' I think about high-level, forward-looking, substantive, and usually longer-term. We are talking about the big picture priorities of the organization, typically answering the 'why' and 'when' questions, not 'operational' or 'tactical,' which are usually lower-level and shorter-term and typically answering the 'how' and 'who' questions. Reviewing the budget annually is a good example. A strategic board would focus on the big picture. To what extent does management's proposed allocation of resources reflect what we talked about during our strategic planning? An operational board, on the other hand, would go through the budget line item by line item and ask specifically about how the funds are being used, for what initiatives, by whom, and where?"

10. What kind of approach to inclusivity have you taken in the past?

Answer: Provide a specific example. Show them you understand the differences between equity, diversity, and inclusion as you tell your story.

"I think of inclusion as the specific steps we are going to take to accomplish the desired optimal mix of diverse people, ultimately to achieve equity and fairness in access for everyone, especially those from groups who traditionally have not benefited from equal access privileges. For our workplace, I made sure that inclusion began with awareness, which was a long journey of discovery into both the value of diversity and exclusionary biases in myself, often invisible for many years. A goal is respectful engagement, listening deeply, and valuing those with differences. Through awareness training and small group discovery explorations, our work teams began the journey to inclusion. Further steps involved engaging everyone in setting priorities and designing initiatives. Structure, direction, reporting, and accountability were all enhanced over several iterations and years by patiently forging consensus around each. A healthy inclusive culture was developed and then maintained through dialogue, orientation, and ongoing education."

11. **What have you done to understand how to remove barriers for marginalized and racialized groups, thereby increasing diversity and inclusivity in an organization?**

Answer: Even if you haven't been personally active in doing something in a professional sense, your answer can demonstrate that you are taking responsibility for your own personal learning. Consider sharing examples from your personal life.

"A fire partially destroyed our residential care building. This rented facility was not purpose-built, nor did it continue to meet the socioeconomic needs of our community. Renovations to the site would be in vain. We immediately worked with the funders to secure a new facility. After three years of work, we have recently opened a new facility for residential high-need clients. This population had been largely marginalized, and attention to their care environment had been abandoned some years ago. Our new facility was designed with an advisory group of patients and families and our trusted partners in local First Nations communities. Our facility has been designed to allow for First Nations ceremony and healing. Our advisory group has also contributed to our re-branding of the site to pick a name that is intentionally inclusive."

Behavioral Questions

Behavioral questions explore how the interviewee has acted in complicated situations and how they make tough decisions.

1. **Describe a recent board agenda item where you held an opposing view to other directors. How was it received? How did you handle it?**

Answer: Demonstrate that you can effectively state your case in the face of conflict or disagreement.

"When I joined this particular board, nobody was following any guidelines, practices, policies, or standards; it was the Wild West! I walked into the boardroom and was told, 'This is how we do things.' Management was openly violating rules and ethical standards, and nobody was holding them accountable. I began by bringing out the policies and standards—especially our values and code of conduct. I was faced with comments like, 'That's not the way we do things.' I had to remind people this IS the way we agreed to do things. I had the corporate secretary review all relevant policies and standards, one at a time, in a series of board meetings. Eventually, with consistency in leadership from the chair and frequent reminders, everyone came together. When we worked together as a team, it was a win-win for everyone. We were finally all on the same page. This took a year from start to finish, when everyone understood what our goals, plan, and future were to look like. Board members and management had forgotten their commitment to integrity. Change is hard, but it was necessary, and the outcome benefited everyone, especially the organization itself."

2. Tell us about a time when you were on a board with someone you did not get along with. What happened?

Answer: Provide a specific example. Show alignment with the organization's mission, vision, and values and the ability to work collaboratively within the culture of the organization.

"I served on a board where one of the board members was constantly ignoring me and was quite rude about it. For a time, I took it personally and got my back up, trying to argue and debate. Then I realized that their personality type was the complete opposite of mine and that evidence-based decision-making was of no interest to them. So, I changed my approach. When engaging that board member, I framed things through the lens of achieving results and cutting red tape. While not ignoring them, I didn't focus on the best practices benchmarking and expert reports but looked them in the eye and cut to the chase—here is the committee's recommendation, and here is what it will achieve. Everything changed, and I've applied that lesson many times since. Different people need different approaches."

3. What one new thing have you learned recently that has made you a better director?

Answer: Bring a curious, respectful, thoughtful, and strategic perspective to your answer.

"Realizing how both 'ESG' and 'EDI' have become so polarizing in boardrooms, and that this can completely cloud rational deliberations and decision-making on issues that really matter to the organization and our stakeholders. By moving away from those labels and focusing on the underlying business benefits instead, we've built consensus on some significant strategic priorities. A small example is reducing waste and energy use. By focusing on cost savings instead of altruistic climate change, all board members more readily signed off so we could move on. Strategically, both the organization and the environment benefited."

4. Tell us about a time when another board member changed your mind on a big decision item.

Answer: Provide a specific example.

"I was dead-set against shutting down in-person branch services to one of our market segments and replacing this with online virtual services. But I was curious to know management's rationale. On the surface, it just seemed to me that our clients really valued and even needed the 'personal touch.' But management was able to show me how virtual services would be able to deliver considerably more 'touch' to the client for a lower cost to them and better efficiencies for us. And my other board colleagues were in agreement with management, so I listened carefully to understand their perspectives on the issues. Employees didn't have to waste so much travel time, and clients rated the services better than before. It took some research and comparators to fully persuade me, but I listened to the evidence and my fellow board members, and I did change my mind!"

5. Tell us about a time you demonstrated respect and thoughtfulness around the board table. What does that look like?

Answer: Share a specific example. If you don't have board experience, look to experiences where you were collaborating with a team.

"Early in the COVID pandemic, when our meetings went virtual, we had a lot of technical challenges. Some board members just had no idea how to use the virtual meeting technology. Even after several meetings, they couldn't connect their device properly, or they were on audio but not video, or video but not audio, then they'd mute and talk … you know! As chair, I had to constantly exercise patience, grace, and respect and often had to call on my colleagues around the board to do the same thing. We even adopted a virtual meeting protocol that explicitly talked about respect and thoughtfulness. I think it has made us better listeners in general, not just virtually."

6. Tell us about a time when you had to explain a complex financial issue.

Answer: That might include how you explained investments to a board member without any expertise or background in investments. If you don't have board experience, spotlight how you explained a financial issue to a peer or leader in an organization. It might be, for example, how you explained the pros and cons of a financial strategy that the human resources leader would like to implement?

"In our financial institution, we had a liquidity issue and so were seeking board approval to securitize some of our mortgages, raise liquidity, and fund new loan growth, which was in demand. We were in an economic boom at the time. Well, I realized that it would be complex to explain how securitization worked, especially since there are 'vanilla' and less vanilla packages to consider, and I was prepared with explanations and metaphors. But then I realized that some board members were not as financially literate as others. Several were less familiar with the liquidity question itself and why we would even want to sell some of our mortgages to another lender. That caused me to rethink the whole financial literacy piece and to begin our financial presentations a couple of steps earlier in their professional development journey. It was a lesson for me—never assume that a board member knows why you're asking for something."

General Questions

Candidates for any board seat should be prepared to answer the following questions. Note that if you're already sitting on other boards or carry a heavy workload, interviewers will be keen to assess whether you really have enough time to devote to their organization.

1. Why are you interested in this role?

2. How did you prepare for today?

3. What jumped out at you from this preparation?

4. What do you know about our organization?

5. What challenges and emerging risks do you see ahead of us?

6. What do you see as the opportunities facing our industry and sector, and how might they affect the way the organization should serve our clients?

7. What strengths do you bring to this board?

8. What are your thoughts on our current financial statements?

9. Can you dedicate sufficient time to your board work?

10. Which committees do you think you can add the most value to, and why?

11. To what extent have you ever dealt with a challenging compensation or talent management situation on your previous boards? If so, what did you do? How did you help the board move through that and collaborate to build consensus?

12. What strategies have you used to engage clients?

And if you've done all the work outlined in this chapter, you'll know exactly how to answer those questions in a way that will help move your candidacy forward.

Afterword

The hunt for a board position isn't like the hunt for any other job. The responsibilities simply aren't the same. At Governance Solutions, we like to think of the board as playing the grand-parent role. Think about the difference between being a parent and a grandparent. As a parent, we are responsible for the day-to-day, hands-on raising of our children. Grandparents, however, provide a higher level of oversight and interaction. So, like a grandparent, board members should not get into the day-to-day operations and details. They are to provide a much higher level of strategic oversight. The extent to which you can demonstrate that you both know and can act on these differences will prove your degree of board readiness.

In collaboration with peers, you'll be expected to bring a high level of experience, new perspectives, and leadership to the organization as it grapples with emerging challenges in the ever-changing global marketplace.

The winners in this equation set themselves apart from the competition. They've reached top-level success in their career. They've built an active network of professional and personal contacts. And they've done all the research and preparation required to craft the perfect board résumé and nail the interview. And, through it all, they've been focused on giving the board what it needs, not what they need for their own career or ego. They've demonstrated that they're the best new partner for an organization's boardroom.

Ready to go? Consider this book your board ready action plan, and start following the steps below to set yourself up for success.

Getting on a Board: Action Plan

Strategy 1: Know Yourself

Conduct an honest and specific assessment of your experience and identify the kind of company you can add the most value to.

- Consider industry and geography.

- Know the answer to this statement: "I can add the most value in this industry, in this location, in these specific ways." (Focus on how you can give the board what they need rather than simply, "I want a board seat.")

- Identify any potential conflicts of interest (real or perceived).

- Manage your expectations.

Strategy 2: Be Board Ready

Being ready when the right opportunity opens up means always having your sights set on what could be next and making the right moves throughout your career.

- Develop and leverage the right professional skills.

- Get some experience reporting to boards and serving on boards (from small to large). All experience is beneficial.

- Chair a committee.

- Keep your director résumé current and customizable.

- Know what boards are looking for in new board members by reading candidate profiles.

- Build your brand.

- Develop compelling stories that support your brand.

Strategy 3: Be Educated

Board members will need to bring business skills and knowledge to the table, including on topics such as financial literacy, risk oversight, and executive compensation. But an education in governance also is critical. The more educated you are in governance, the more likely you'll have the skills that boards are looking for as they fill vacant seats.

- Obtain your designation—Pro.Dir, C.Dir, ICD.D.

- Keep your certification up to date.

- Stay on top of what's new in governance.

Strategy 4: Know the Organization and Your Fit Within It
You need to evaluate the board as much as they need to evaluate you.

- Study the company. Understand and assess their strategy, financial health, leadership team, board members, approach to governance, and governance structure.

- Determine whether they have a governance ranking.

- Assess their board profile and determine whether you would fill any gaps by comparing your profile against their needs and gaps.

- Rate your fit with their board.

- Build your stories to prove your fit.

- Ask for the seat!

Strategy 5: Be a Networker
By far, the No. 1 way to get a board seat is through networking.

- Cast a wide net and build relationships.

- Fine-tune your LinkedIn profile and be active by connecting with others, commenting on their posts, and sharing your own thought leadership.

- Join associations.

- Work your contacts.

- Get references and ask for endorsements.

- Contact board search firms, but don't rely solely on them.

- Check industry and company websites.

That first board position can be the toughest one to get. Sometimes, having nonprofit board work first or having worked with boards in your paid employment helps you go for the for-profit positions. Whether you're in the starting blocks looking for your first board position or looking to add to the wealth of experience you already have, the best step you can take to set yourself up as the most appealing candidate for that desired board position is to prepare. Do your homework, and then go and get that seat.

Endnotes

1   "2023 U.S. Spencer Stuart Board Index," Spencer Stuart, accessed Oct. 9, 2023, https://www.spencerstuart.com/research-and-insight/us-board-index.

2   Boivie, Steven, et al. "Serving on Boards Helps Executives Get Promoted," *Harvard Business Review*, May 20, 2016, https://hbr.org/2016/05/serving-on-boards-helps-executives-get-promoted.

3   "Missing Pieces Report: A board diversity census of women and underrepresented racial and ethnic groups on Fortune 500 boards, 7th edition," Alliance for Board Diversity and Deloitte, released June 8, 2021, https://www2.deloitte.com/us/en/pages/center-for-board-effectiveness/articles/missing-pieces-report-board-diversity.html.

4   "Representation of Women on Boards of Directors, 2018,"
    Statistics Canada, released March 3, 2021, https://www150.
    statcan.gc.ca/n1/daily-quotidien/210323/dq210323d-eng.htm.

5   Institutional Shareholder Services, Inc., "Gender Parity on Boards
    Around the World," Harvard Law School Forum on Corporate
    Governance, January 5, 2017, https://corpgov.law.harvard.
    edu/2017/01/05/gender-parity-on-boards-around-the-world/.

6   Michael Hatcher and Weldom Latham, "States are Leading
    the Charge to Corporate Boards: Diversify!", Harvard Law
    School Forum on Corporate Governance, https://corpgov.
    law.harvard.edu/2020/05/12/states-are-leading-the-charge-t
    o-corporate-boards-diversify/.

7   Melancon, J. Merritt, "Consumer buying power is more diverse
    than ever," *UGA Today*, Aug. 11, 2021, https://news.uga.edu/
    selig-multicultural-economy-report-2021/.

8   "Diversity wins: How inclusion matters," McKinsey & Co., released
    May 19, 2020, https://www.mckinsey.com/featured-insights/
    diversity-and-inclusion/diversity-wins-how-inclusion-matters.

9   Venkataramani, Swetha, "The ESG Imperative: 7 Factors
    for Finance Leaders to Consider," Gartner, released June
    19, 2021, https://www.gartner.com/smarterwithgartner/
    the-esg-imperative-7-factors-for-finance-leaders-to-consider.

10 "2019 AFLAC CSR Survey," Aflac, accessed Aug. 22, 2022,
    https://www.aflac.com/docs/about-aflac/csr-survey-asset
    s/2019-aflac-csr-infographic-and-survey.pdf.

11 "2023 Job Seekers: What They Want," *CareerBuilder.
    com*, Oct. 10, 2023, https://b2b.careerbuilder.com/
    CB_What_Jobseekers_Want_2023.

12 "2020 Recruiter Nation Survey," Jobvite, released Oct. 13,
    2020, https://www.jobvite.com/wp-content/uploads/2020/10/
    Jobvite-RecruiterNation-Report-Final.pdf.

13 "About LinkedIn," LinkedIn, accessed Feb. 16, 2024, https://about.linkedin.com/.

14 "Display Order of Skills," LinkedIn, accessed Aug. 22, 2022, https://www.linkedin.com/help/linkedin/answer/a568137/display-order-of-skills?lang=en.

15 "How Americans Prepare for Interviews," JDP, accessed Aug. 22, 2022, https://www.jdp.com/blog/how-to-prepare-for-interviews-2020/.

About the Authors

Dr. Debra L. Brown

Debra was five years old when her father sat her behind the wheel of the family tractor, pointed at a tree across the field, and told her to drive straight at it, never taking her eye off the mark. It was her first lesson in vision and strategy: know where you're going, how to get there, and stay focused. Today, she is a globally respected thought leader and the founder, president, and CEO of Governance Solutions.

Under Debra's leadership, GSI developed a comprehensive, principles-based governance system that has been adopted by organizations, governments, and not-for-profits around the world. It was also the foundation for The Directors College, The Professional Director Education and Certification Program®, and other governance education and university-accredited certification programs.

Prior to founding Governance Solutions, Debra twice served as a CEO and sat on the board of several organizations, including as Board Chair and Governance Committee Chair. As a result, she is uniquely qualified as a governance advisor, with the ability to see issues from both sides of the boardroom table.

Debra has co-authored four books and written dozens of articles and publications on corporate governance. She also writes a column for *The Financial Gazette* and regularly contributes to *Ethical Boardroom*, a globally recognized corporate governance periodical.

Equally prolific outside work, Debra is an enthusiastic painter, poet, and musician. A Professional Director and member of The Institute of Corporate Directors, Debra also holds a doctorate in leadership and a master of divinity from Gordon-Conwell Theological Seminary, where she graduated magma cum laude.

CONNECT WITH DEBRA

Follow her on your favorite social media platforms today.

ProfessionalDirector.com

David A. H. Brown

The son of two bankers, David grew up listening to business problems around the dining room table – and how to solve them. It's been his passion ever since. Today, David is Canada's leading thinker, speaker, writer, and practitioner in corporate governance.

As executive vice president and the team's lead consultant, David has helped countless organizations improve their governance and board effectiveness. He cares deeply about corporations and their innate capacity to do good—as well as their inherent risk of doing bad. His life's work is helping leaders make better choices for themselves and everyone they touch.

David's also co-founded over a dozen board governance education programs, including university-accredited certification programs, The Professional Director Education and Certification Program®, the Directors College, and more.

Prior to joining Governance Solutions in 1995, David had a distinguished twenty-year career in Canada's financial services industry. As an insolvency specialist, he learned hard lessons about the necessity for good corporate governance—and how badly things can go in its absence.

David holds a B.Comm (Hons) from Queen's University in addition to Chartered Director and Professional Director designations in corporate governance. He's also served as an accredited faculty member of several universities, including the Universities of St. Michael's College, Toronto; Universities of Regina and Saskatchewan, Saskatchewan; and McMaster University, Hamilton.

David has co-authored several books and written dozens of articles and publications on corporate governance. An avid college football fan, he spends every Saturday afternoon in the fall cheering on the Alabama Crimson Tide.

About Governance Solutions

As globally respected leaders in all things governance, we help boards and executives understand their role in governance so they can succeed and their organizations can win. Unlock the full potential of your board and governance system and optimize your governance through our superior, integrated portfolio of products and services.

GovernanceSolutions.ca

Other Books by the Authors

Governance Solutions: The Ultimate Guide to Competence and Confidence in the Boardroom

Today's board members need more tools, not more rules!

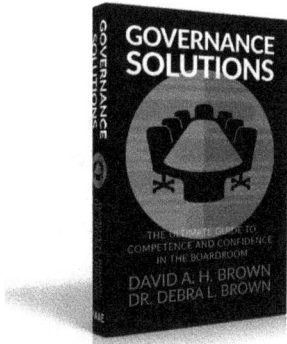

Governance Solutions: The Ultimate Guide to Competence and Confidence in the Boardroom is chock-full of governance tools that make the complex seem simple and bring order to the chaos.

This is not just a book *about governance*; it tells you how to *do governance*.

Authors David A. H. Brown and Dr. Debra L. Brown deliver

- proven governance solutions: this book is a single source—the ultimate guide—for solving your governance problems.

- access: *Governance Solutions* includes almost seventy governance concepts and tools that are unique only to this book.

- competence and confidence: the book covers the broad spectrum of governance issues from governance structure and process through boardroom leadership, culture, and behavior.

- answers! this book tells you not only what works but, just as importantly, what does not work in governance.

With so many spotlights trained on corporate boards, there could hardly be a better moment for hands-on, cutting-edge guidance on how directors can power success—and avoid traps. David and Debra Brown are world-class experts; their new book earns a place on director desks everywhere.

Stephen Davis, Ph.D.
Associate Director and Senior Fellow
Harvard Law School Programs on Corporate Governance
and Institutional Investors

Governing in Scary Times: The Board's Roadmap for Governing Through and Beyond an Emergency

COVID-19 threw the world into scary times!

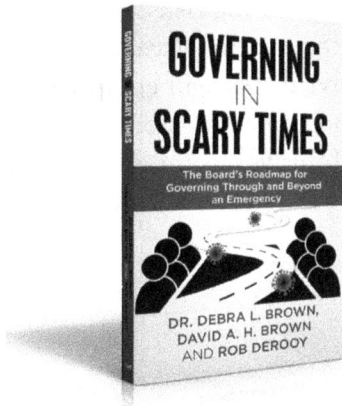

If the global pandemic taught us anything, it's that all organizations need a strategy to manage in a crisis. In *Governing in Scary Times*, authors Dr. Debra L. Brown, David A. H. Brown, and Rob DeRooy offer a step-by-step plan to prepare your board to provide direction for your company and reinforce your stakeholder confidence.

With a combined seventy-five years of experience governing companies and boards, the authors guide you through a process that will prepare you to answer key questions:

- Where are we headed?

- What obstacles and opportunities might we face along the way?

- Who will do what?

- What are the boundaries and guidelines?

- How will we resource our efforts?

Governing in Scary Times is your boardroom roadmap to navigating extreme challenges in your business. From developing a strategic plan to assessing risks and policies to getting and keeping the right people in place, the authors provide practical and proven advice that will equip your company to survive scary times—and come out stronger on the other side.

Another crisis is (always) coming. Use the strategies in *Governing in Scary Times* to ensure your organization is prepared.

ESG Matters

Save the Planet, Empower People, and Outperform the Competition starting today!

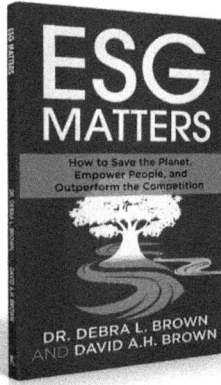

We only have one planet.

Individually and corporately, we are all stewards of the natural environment, but we have not protected, nurtured, or renewed it as well as we should have.

In ESG Matters, authors Dr. Debra L. Brown and David A. H. Brown challenge the thinking that businesses operate in a vacuum, separate from the environment. Maintaining a focus on environment, social, and governance (ESG) places an organization a step above those that don't consider the ethics of good business.

ESG goes beyond corporate social responsibility that holds an organization accountable. ESG criteria creates visible metrics for the organization.

ESG Matters helps readers:

- examine their beliefs to make financial and investment decisions thoughtfully and deliberately.

- understand how to use their purchasing power to protect and renew the environment.

- recognize the true impact of their spending decisions.

- influence public perception and ultimately boost their bottom line.

Virtually There

Dos and Don'ts for Planning, Chairing, and Holding
Virtual Board and Annual General Meetings

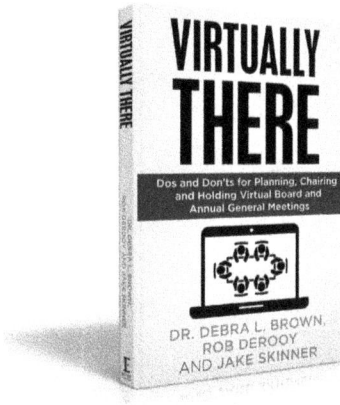

Authors Dr. Debra L. Brown, Rob DeRooy, and Jake
Skinner draw from their years of governance and technical
experience to share best practices that strengthen unity and
community for your organization.

Discover how to optimize your virtual meetings by

- Creating healthy engagement and spirited communi-
cation to solve issues at hand.

- Drawing out people who tend to hold back and quell-
ing others who tend to dominate, so all feel heard and
respected.

- Establishing agreed-upon guidelines that foster progress
and growth.

"Pragmatic, helpful and full of great learnings! A must-read for every leader who is serious about ensuring excellence for their virtual board meetings and AGMs!"

—David Bodnarchuk, FCPA FCA,
President, ElectionBuddy Inc.

Start tapping into greater levels of success, regardless of where you meet. Available wherever books are sold.

Earn Your Professional Director® Designation

Conceptual Model: **Why Do Boards Exist.**

A world-class, online director education program where you can build competence and confidence in governance while you earn a Pro.Dir designation.

Whether you have a little, some, or a lot of governance experience, this program will build the confidence, skills, knowledge, and competence in governance you need to make it in today's complex boardroom.

As a certified Professional Director®, you will enjoy internationally-recognized status as a graduate of one of the world's leading director education programs.

Start earning your ProDir® designation today with a free introductory session—no obligation or credit card required. You'll instantly see the value and be one step closer to internationally-recognized certification!

ProfessionalDirector.com

www.ingramcontent.com/pod-product-compliance
Lightning Source LLC
Chambersburg PA
CBHW070657190326
41458CB00053B/6913/J